Managing for Quality
in the
Service Sector

Managing for Quality in the Service Sector

Edited by

WILLEM F.G. MASTENBROEK

Copyright © Basil Blackwell Ltd 1991

First published 1991

Basil Blackwell Ltd
108 Cowley Road, Oxford, OX4 1JF, UK

Basil Blackwell, Inc.
3 Cambridge Center
Cambridge, Massachusetts 02142, USA

British Library Cataloguing in Publication Data

A CIP catalogue record for this book is available from the British Library.

Library of Congress Cataloging in Publication Data

Managing for quality in the service sector/edited by Willem F.G. Mastenbroek.
    p.   cm.
  Includes index.
  ISBN 0–631–17499–0
  1. Service industries—Management. 2. Service industries—Quality control.
I. Mastenbroek, W.F.G.
HD9980.5.M342 1991
658.5'62—dc20
90-2316 CIP

Typeset in 10½ on 12 pt Plantin
by Photo·graphics, Honiton, Devon
Printed in Great Britain by T J Press Ltd., Padstow, Cornwall

Contents

PART V STEP-BY-STEP PLANS AND PROGRAMMES

Contributors from the Holland Consulting Group

Ing. Gé Brand Mechanical engineer and qualified lecturer in economics. Active as management consultant since 1954. Has been in charge of many large reorganization and strategic planning projects, mainly in government organizations. Activities also involve quality programmes, management development, cultural change processes, and quality improvement in the sector of energy distribution.

Drs Pieterjan van Delden Active as management consultant since 1976. Has been involved in innovation projects and industrial enterprises, social aspects of automation, quality of labour and improving the quality of services. Has published several books and writes regularly for management journals.

Drs Jeroen M. Drontmann Active as a management consultant since 1985. Work primarily concerned with quality improvement, conflict management and negotiating, cooperation issues and team development, and cultural change.

Drs Gerco C. Ezerman Consults in the areas of quality improvement, management development, company training, improving cooperation and (de)centralization issues.

Prof. dr Hein W.C. van der Hart Active in the areas of business-to-business marketing and service marketing in industry and the not-for-profit sector. Professor of marketing at the Eindhoven University of Technology, Department of Business Administration. Author of several books and articles concerning industrial marketing and service marketing.

Drs Arjan J. Kampfraath Active in the consulting areas of policy and strategy, quality improvement and information management. Associated with the Erasmus University Rotterdam on a part-time basis.

Mr Leo A.F.M. Kerklaan Has held various functions in financial and industrial organizations, and was Head of Corporate Quality Audit at Fokker Ltd. Active as an internal and external consultant for the past seven years. Has published several books on quality (including quality in framework and quality in motion) and a number of articles. Fields of interest are strategic management, company audit and quality control.

Drs Paul P. Kloosterboer Active as a consultant in the fields of quality improvement and human resources development. Has published several articles on quality improvement and management consulting.

Dr Willem F.G. Mastenbroek Has been working as a management consultant since 1970. Activities concern the management of structural and cultural innovations in organizations. Projects have concentrated on quality improvement; has developed various programmes and instruments in this area. Has held part-time positions at universities in The Netherlands for several years. Author of several books, including *Conflict Management and Organization Development* (Wiley, 1987) and *Negotiate!* (Basil Blackwell, 1989), and over 100 articles on organizational theory and the management of organizational innovation.

Prof. ir drs Willem J. Vrakking Active as management consultant since 1971. Major consulting areas are the development of strategies and the design of new structural concepts in relation to new technologies. Specialist in the management of organizational innovation projects. Professor of Innovation and Internal Entrepreneurship at the Economic Faculty of the Erasmus University Rotterdam.

Prof. dr Arjan J. van Weele Areas of experience are strategic management, business review, business logistics, purchasing and supply management. Part-time engagement as professor at the Eindhoven University of Technology, Faculty of Industrial Engineering, teaching courses in purchasing management and strategic sourcing. Has published widely (over 50 articles and several books) on strategic management, business logistics, and purchasing and supply management.

Introduction

WILLEM F.G. MASTENBROEK

This book was written by a group of management consultants of the Holland Consulting Group. Each of these consultants is involved with projects concerning improvement of the quality of service. Some of these projects are in the service sector, some in central departments of production companies. Other experiences are related to improving the service aspects in industrial products. Within the Holland Consulting Group these consultants work together in the Product Group Quality Improvement. Their experiences and ideas have been collected in this volume.

The field of quality improvement in the service sector is undergoing rapid developments. At first the service sector clearly lagged behind industry, but the arrears have been made up rapidly. Today we can see that the industrial sector is beginning to reap rewards from the experiences and ideas developed in the service sector; the lag is changing into a lead! One major cause is the dynamics of the service sector – its expansion and competition. The most important reason is that quality and customer orientation have traditionally been considered essential tasks by management in the service sector.

This book consists of five parts. In part I, 'Developments and conditions', we present a survey of the driving forces behind the increasing importance of quality and customer orientation in society and organizations. Part II, 'Supporting models and techniques', provides several aids for analysing and solving quality problems. Part III, 'Experiences and problem areas', describes cases and experiences. Part IV, 'Motivation and improved cooperation', describes the importance of communication, management style and mode of cooperation for quality improvement. Furthermore, it indicates how desired changes in these areas can be realized. Part V, 'Step-by-step plans and programmes', aims to give concrete and specific recommendations to provide structure and support for the process of quality improvement. This last part also provides an integrating framework for the previous parts. All parts have a practical orientation, and all chapters contain a host of examples and brief case descriptions.

Simultaneously the book provides integrating theoretical frameworks. These are practice oriented, and intended to classify experiences. However, they are also aimed at understanding what it is all about, which are the most powerful levers in the multitude of interesting ideas, experiences and techniques. In this way we hope to contribute to a faster and more precise development of this very important field.

This book is an extended and improved edition of a Dutch original. Only the cooperation and efforts of many others have made it possible to achieve this.

A special word of thanks is due to the clients of the Holland Consulting Group, who confronted us with a wide variety of experiences. Without them and without their cooperation and active involvement there would be no book.

I wish to thank Margaret Oattes for translating much of the Dutch text into English; also Brian Goodale, Basil Blackwell copy-editor, who further improved the accessibility of the text.

PART I

Developments and conditions

1

The breakthrough of service in industry: new forms of service by manufacturers

PIETERJAN VAN DELDEN

INTRODUCTION

In an empty factory building, there are rows and rows of biscuit-tin-like vehicles. These are mobile dairy shops, repurchased by their manufacturer Spijkstaal, a company in northern Holland, for the purpose of reselling them to shopkeepers after they have been renovated. This is a solution born of necessity: only in this way can these mobile shops be passed on from those owners whose businesses are going well to those who are less well off. The former are able to purchase a new vehicle, and the latter can get theirs for a reasonable price. Spijkstaal is purely a steel company, but has nevertheless set up this trade because it is the only way its product can find continual outlets. Necessity is the mother of invention here!

Production people do not like trade. A classic example is the remark made by a former Ford employee about his product: 'This is a fantastic truck, there simply *must* be a market for it!' The Ford Transcontinental was indeed a first class vehicle, but it was too heavy and too expensive for the European market. So production was stopped.

This lack of understanding shows the strained relationship between production and sales, deeply embedded in all industrial companies. Boards and managers accept this with shrugged shoulders. Spijkstaal's exceptional emergency solution was inevitable, because its own market segment threatened to clog up. Yet it is often these practical survival solutions, born of necessity, which are the forerunners of a new trend. More and more industrial companies are making a virtue of necessity, and organize all kinds of activities in order to meet their potential clients' needs more efficiently.

INDUSTRIAL SERVICE

Industry's conversion to service – the term for this development – now affects most production companies to a greater or lesser extent. Sales sense and market intuition have come to score high in management, even in the classical industrial sector.

There are three elements in industrial service: direct support of the product, information and after-sales service. Today, it is self-evident that modern companies wrap up a physical product in supporting services. Agreements are made beforehand about types of product, possible accessories, delivery times and methods of payment. The low-interest loans offered by car dealers show how far one can go in this area. On a larger scale as well, service is frequently a discussion point. Sometimes manufacturers can only get a large order from a developing country if they also arrange the financing. Then there is the information provided about the product itself (see the infamous non-manuals for computers), advice, technical support and training when products are installed and brought on line. Then finally there is after-sales service or field service: guarantees, maintenance contracts, supply of service parts, help with repairs, expansion or replacement, and updating of software, which is often built in. The follow-up or after-sales service itself represents considerable business.

More service in industry means that this add-on package is more finely regulated, and is adjusted to the needs of specific groups of customers. If necessary, extra functions are added to make this fine regulation possible. This requires considerable internal tuning and flexibility. The medium companies are often the first to learn how to do it. Take for example the graphic sector. Dozens of printing shops have expanded their pre-press departments considerably in recent years. The actual printing process itself has already been perfected thanks to the high-quality equipment available on the market, so there is not much to gain by trying to compete on this point. The main issue now is to anticipate customer wishes: reduction of delivery times, rapid communication, sometimes even keeping tabs on the customer's stock oneself, or correcting texts. There is, however, a next step: make design or logo proposals, suggest company colours, and think along with the customer from the start about house style. In this way, the printer takes over part of the work of the designer and artist, and integrates it into the production process. Service is relieving the customer of coordination problems by offering him as many functions as possible in one integrated package.

FORCED FLEXIBILITY

Small and medium companies have a comparative advantage in following market wishes flexibly and actively. This is sometimes in the nature of the industry in question (consider the success that the personal computer brought to small computer manufacturers); sometimes the older industrial sectors have to learn the hard way. In the ready-made clothing industry, only the small and very flexible manufacturers are able to keep up the fight. In Western Europe, only those companies that react promptly to current fashion can survive and flourish under this forced flexibility.

An example of the latter in The Netherlands is Albert Westerman Knitwear Fashions, which made it on that basis. The company bears little resemblance now to an old-fashioned knitted goods factory. Instead it presents itself to its clients as a service company. Delivery times have been reduced dramatically: ten years ago it took four weeks to make jumpers to order; a few years ago it took a week; and nowadays it is possible to take the product home with you on the same day! The trick has been to link design computers with production. Customers arrive with their sketches and their colour needs. They are present when this information is fed into and processed by the computer, which produces a punched tape; this is used to start the knitting machines working immediately. This service is very nice for the readers of women's magazines, who can take delivery of the desired jumper or sweater within a few days. But there is more: most important are the nearness of the market, the closeness to the customer, the ability to translate a new trend into a design immediately. Being able to talk to the customer – that's what makes all the difference. Westerman treats his designers (steady freelancers) very well, and lets them go on trips to Paris or Milan to absorb the newest fads. On the other hand, all possible steps are taken to prevent designers and production planners from growing away from production. These functions are placed on a management island, a group of offices and design studios in the factory itself, separated from the surrounding workshops only by high windows. There is permanent visual contact, and as a result there is hardly any difference in status between sales, planning and production. Service is not an activity separate from production, but reacts to production directly.

EXPERIENCE IN SERVICE SKILLS

More service in industry is supported in part by the people who have direct contact with customers. The key aspects here are thinking along with the customer, communication, solving problems and building up relationships. It is not surprising therefore that some industrial markets are being entered by specialist service companies. Such companies have the experience and the attitudes necessary for approaching the public in a helpful way.

Network 3 is a subsidiary of the Randstad group which has addressed itself to the guarding and security of private houses in The Netherlands. Originally this market was reserved for installation companies and manufacturers, who tried to sell their hardware (hinges and locks, sensors, alarm bells and sirens etc.) directly to the public. In effect it was a product market, but not a satisfactory one. J.E. van der Stoop, marketing manager with Network 3, established that these products did not meet customers' requirements and so left a gap in the market.

> It is precisely in the private sector that things often go wrong when people try the do-it-yourself approach. There is a lot of cheap material on the market, so it is tempting to buy an alarm set for Dfl 300 (£100) at the local DIY shop and do the job yourself. The shops and the installation firms prefer to sell, that is to turn over material which needs little or no maintenance. In the first year (the guarantee year) things usually go well, but after that there are often problems. A small renovation means an extra cable has to be installed. The equipment gets older and often more sensitive and goes off sooner. Or a new pet is bought and it has different habits. After a few instances of false alarm, your next door neighbour no longer comes to check, or the police will start to talk about charging you for coming round. People then often start to fiddle about with the installation themselves, and sooner or later the supplier has to be called in. There is a lot of fuss, and less security. That's why we don't sell any installations. Instead we sell security subscriptions. This means that after consulting the customer, we install sensors in the house which will set off a so-called quiet alarm if danger threatens. The alarm centre at Network 3 calls back, and informs the police if the secret customer code is not provided.

This form of security is well established for companies. Now Network 3 hopes that a series of small readjustments (simple operation, no outside sirens, reasonable costs etc.) will make it attractive and manageable for the private customer. As van der Stoop puts it:

> The advantage is that there are no high procurement costs or repair costs, because the installation remains our property. The customer only pays an initial entry fee and the subscription fees, and no longer has to worry whether the police will come or not. For elderly people in particular, it is important to feel that their house is well guarded and that they can sleep in peace.

So, technology has become subservient to the service formula. The customer pays for the equipment, but its care is someone else's responsibility. Network 3 sells not security installations, but security!

LINKING UP THE CUSTOMER

The success of a service company in a market originally reserved for products shows that the art of providing services is sometimes more important than manufacturing clever products. The creative designers in the graphic industry, the communication designers at Westerman Knitwear and the customer-oriented fitters at Network 3 serve as models for the new industrial trade group: the product developers who can translate customer wishes directly into design and technology. The more companies succeed in cultivating this group within their own organization, the easier it becomes for them to retain their relationships with the customers. But there is more than communication and creativity. It is precisely those industrial companies converted to service that are characterized by high investments in mechanization and automation. Westerman Knitwear is already close to computer integrated manufacturing (CIM); in the flexible graphic companies, it will not be long before text and illustrations are processed and transmitted via computers, up to and including the actual printing.

This conversion to service emerges most strongly in the tendency to link up customers to the company's computer system. Network 3 receives its alarm signals via the telephone, after which they are interpreted and passed on to the alarm centre by the computer. In this way the central exchange officer knows immediately which customer is involved, where exactly in the house the prowler has been noticed, and which police station should be called.

Printing companies have their texts transmitted directly from the client's computer to their own computer by phone line. The Americans have invented the term 'electronic linkages' for this system, and some management consultants trumpet around that any company which does not have all its customers and suppliers bound to its computer within three years will be finished.

Some European companies provide good examples of the competitive advantages gained from telematics. The Italian fashion manufacturer Benetton cuts costs by limiting the size of retail outlets to a minimum number of square feet, which can however be stocked at a fantastic rate. This is only possible thanks to an extensive computer network which informs the suppliers immediately and precisely as to requirements in patterns and colours.

Something similar is also done by Custom Vêtements Associates, the American branch of a French clothing manufacturer. Certain retail shops in the US have the equipment necessary to translate sizes given by customers into codes, which are sent to the central computer in New York overnight. From there they are transmitted by satellite to the factory computer in Strasburg. The following day a laser cuts the material to size and the ordered clothes are produced. The order can be shipped within four days; previously it took many weeks to order and produce made-to-measure clothing. This is a form of conversion to service which radically ties together all the steps in the process from client to factory and back.

FACILITY MANAGEMENT

To what extent is conversion to service reserved for small and medium companies? The examples above suggest that, from now on, large companies will lose the battle for the greatest customer orientation and flexibility. How can one meet the individual wishes of thousands of customers simultaneously? This is primarily a problem for those large industrial companies that grew big in production and technology. In general Philips Electronics has a good reputation in this area, but it is regularly subject to criticism for its lack of customer friendliness and market intuition. In the computer area its successes are moderate; even in the area it knows best – consumer electronics – it is going through a hard time. Yet the company has a lot of experience in combining production and service.

Philips Sales Organization supplies complete systems for furnishing buildings. H. Keizer, director of this group, has noticed the trend to service conversion for some time:

> Traditionally we worked from a collection of technologies which went together logically. We still do, but for years now we have been working at stepping out at the top end of the market in an integrated fashion. In its extreme form this might entail the following. In a city, you are responsible for public health. You need a building which is suitable for nursing and everything that goes with it. Meals must be cooked; visitors enter; you need beds, an emergency first aid department, operating theatres, some laboratories. You need the means to provide health care. In an extreme case you ask yourself why you should have all the worry about such a building. You ask someone else to build it for you, including all the trimmings; even to run it for you, so you can concentrate on your own profession. That is the current trend in the top

of the market. Smaller companies also have these needs, but none of them is able to do it individually. So they set up industrial estates, where such facilities are available for all. This is how facility management starts. As a manufacturer you can no longer afford to supply only some hardware, or only software, or maintenance. You have to start thinking in terms of the concept, and offer the whole range. Thinking is going more and more along the lines of 'I need a function.' This function has to be sound, reliable and carried out as cheaply as possible. There is no point in engaging in all kinds of technical specifications prematurely, for that would be sub-optimization.

REALIZING FUNCTIONS

This way of working is suitable not just for large spectacular projects, but also for smaller ones. The trick is to achieve an exact agreement with the customer about the function that Philips as the main contractor must realize. This is also possible in small projects. One example is Climate Contract, which had Philips develop a network for the security of buildings by remote control. Keizer reports:

> To achieve this we built an alarm centre, to which about 100 buildings all over the country are now connected by telephone lines and sensors. These buildings are managed centrally. In this way, a small company with local subsidiaries can nevertheless cover a broad territory. They no longer need local maintenance departments: the alarm centre transmits on demand the information on the status of elevators, ventilators, generators and temperatures, and if necessary a fitter is sent. All mechanical and electrical installations in the building are linked to the system. These could be the sunshades, the air conditioning, the escalators or the lighting, you name it.

The conversion to service in the supply of professional systems by Philips is mainly realized by the development of complete systems. To this end, Philips Nederland has created a Projects Bureau which concerns itself exclusively with thinking along with the customer. Of course, new technology is not developed for each project. More often it is a matter of cleverly combining existing elements. Keizer is pragmatic on this point:

> Real custom work is far too costly. It's like saying 'I need a car with such and such specifications, and I will have it made to order.' That is out of the question. We mainly use existing products and systems. If we need lamps, then a whole batch goes into boxes, packed here and unpacked there. The important thing is to build in the correct products, and not get bogged down in only one kind of approach, e.g. only air conditioning or only lighting. These two things interact, and this interaction gets so complicated that constructors look for people who can figure it all out and who are willing to take

the final responsibility. And that is much more important than the question of whether it costs a penny more or a penny less. This applies to buildings, but equally to something like a production process. Therefore, instead of risking sub-optimization by aiming for the best in every component area, you should put the whole first.

SPECIALIST ISLANDS

Keizer is still of the opinion that technology will continue to play an important part. Particularly where innovation is concerned, new developments can come from various quarters:

> Research comes up with new ideas which may or may not be taken up by product development groups, which pass them on to manufacturing and the market. That is one way. The compact disk was generated by research, and the market took it up. Other things come at us from the market because there is a need for them. If the Minister of Transport starts talking about toll tunnels and road pricing, then that did not come from technology, but from her need to have a tunnel financed in a certain way. Government does not want attendants punching tickets, so we go to work. Or the department responsible for government buildings says to us: 'We want to do something about energy control and we already have done a lot of things, but nothing about the lighting. Can you help us there? If you can show us that we can cut our costs in a certain time, then we are prepared to invest money and go ahead with it.' We investigated that matter, but could not offer them anything using our current range of products, so we developed a special product for them which meets their typical requirements. We are currently installing low-energy office lighting systems in some 200 government buildings together with the ministry's own fitters.

Here too it is a question of the exact translation of wishes into design, technology and production. On this point, Philips has learned that the value of the customer-oriented product developers mentioned earlier cannot be stressed enough. The demands made on this group are high, so that mainly well-educated personnel are employed in this kind of function, where design, technology and communication are equally important. As Keizer suggests, it is a matter not only of educational levels but also of maintaining relationships:

> If you want to sell analysing equipment to a laboratory, then you need an analytical chemist. He must be skilled in the process alongside the customer who has to use it. He has to know what specialists are doing, to know the profession really well. He must demonstrate the equipment and help the buyer, including with the decision to buy or not. So, for each market, for each application, you need a specialism that connects properly with the customer's

company culture. This market really consists of many separate specialist islands: a building island, a hospital island, a cinema island, a laboratory island. The people on these islands know each other, meet each other at conferences, read the same professional journals, and have often completed their studies under the same professor. That means a bond, and it also has a function. At present we are working on several projects at a government institute. The people have, in many cases, studied under the same professor, and it is pure chance that one has ended up in Philips employ and the other with the government. It could just as easily have been the other way around. It is these networks that we must be part of.

2

Who cares about quality? Organizational conditions and motivation

WILLEM F.G. MASTENBROEK

INTRODUCTION

Schiphol is a prizewinner. For several years in a row, the magazines *Executive Travel* and *Business Traveller* have placed the Dutch airport at the top of the list after comparative research. How does this airport achieve its high-quality service? One example is in the methods of the Operational Service, which have changed towards working in permanent groups with steady colleagues. In the old situation, people were grouped more or less at random, and the main priority was getting the schedule completed. So the relationships between people were quite loose; when at work, they were only interested in their own part of the job. Terminal manager J.M. Abbink says of the new system: 'It is very clear that working in groups, which is new to the staff, creates a strong unity. People are trying much more than before to make something of it together, and if possible to do better than the other teams. It's just positive competition!'

This is one of the ways in which companies attempt to create a new spirit and increased dedication. In recent years a considerable arsenal of insights has become available. A few elements return frequently: small autonomous units, shared values, informal style, customer orientation, continual quality improvement and innovating ability. In addition, there are so many ideas and findings that we are beginning to lose the wood for the trees. In particular it remains unclear how to achieve lasting *motivation* of employees for matters like continual quality improvement and customer orientation. This is a question of the underlying *driving forces*. This chapter will address that question.

STIMULATING CONDITIONS

This chapter intends to show that generating dedication and motivation is connected with influencing the tension balances in the relations between units. Organizational units have joint interests, but they also have separate interests. They focus on consolidating and strengthening their own position in relation to other units. Sometimes they strive for more authority and responsibility. At the same time units are interdependent. They are part of a larger whole. Without this larger whole they would become too isolated. They frequently need the power of the totality. Without it their chances of survival would diminish. This phenomenon can squander, fragment and fritter away human energies in ongoing struggles. It can also stimulate and motivate. Motivating conditions are related to productive rivalries and tension balances between units. Figure 2.1 reflects the tension balance between autonomy and interdependency.

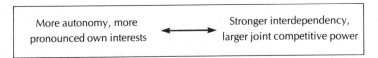

FIGURE 2.1 Tension balance

This dual nature of relations can become a vital source of energy and vitality. However, if the balance tilts too much towards mutual dependency, an organization can become sluggish and complacent; if too much towards self-interest, then insecurity and aggressiveness will become dominant. It is not enough to achieve a certain equilibrium between the two impulses; they must be strengthened and encouraged.

The heart of organizational vitality is a balanced articulation of both interdependency and autonomy. This tension is a source of energy. The better we understand how different organizational changes and interventions influence the tension between autonomy and interdependency, the greater our chance of effectively mobilizing this source of energy.[1]

---

[1] It is fascinating to see how both theory and practice struggle with this inherent tension. In theory we find two schools of thinking: the action and the system perspectives. Each school concentrates on a different aspect of organizations; system

We will now examine from four different angles how organizational conditions and incentives can influence this balance and contribute to motivation. We will see that seemingly separate changes and actions all fit in with this autonomy and interdependency concept. The four perspectives are:

Strategy Internal and external policy in terms of own core activities and goals; not merely aimed at markets and products, but also directing identity, style of functioning and vision of management and organization.

Structure The composition of the organization in units and levels of task areas and authority, as well as the procedures and systems which regulate relations between units.

Culture Behavioural patterns, including management style and ways of cooperation and decision making.

Information Output data, quality indicators and other data supplied by the information systems on the performance of the organization.

Strategy

A shared identity and a well-developed sense of 'our company' are strong binding agents. Several large companies have set down their objectives and their mission in a creed. They go to great lengths to motivate their employees to support this creed. Various possibilities are available, for example the colourful history of the company or the special quality of its products. Every company is sure to have some traits from which identity and pride can be derived. This identity can be strengthened by a house style, but also for example by selecting employees who fit in. The issue is generally an endless confirmation and profiling of the organization's values. This entails more than imprinting mottos and slogans. In this manner companies attempt to fulfil the strong emotional needs of their employees. However, we might hesitate: is this not questionable indoctrination? That kind of doubt is not felt in large Japanese companies; and many Western companies also consciously develop the binding power of shared values. It is significant that Peters

thinking focuses more on cooperation, while the action perspective is more suited to rival interests. Unfortunately, treating these two aspects in different bodies of theory detracts from the foremost characteristic of organizations, that is their dual nature. They are both cooperative and competitive, both parties and systems, both markets and clans, both arenas and sets of complementary functions (Mastenbroek, 1987).

and Waterman (1982) award shared values a central place in their well-known study of excellent organizations. They outline seven levers for success: the so-called 7S model. The prime position in this model is reserved for the S of shared values!

A common identity is sometimes enhanced by certain symbols, logos and a pronounced house style. Organizations try to designate their identity clearly and capture it in a strong formula. AKZO Chemicals has a new emblem. A large department store, V&D, has adopted a new house style. DSM, a Dutch chemical company, is running a campaign with the motto 'We have a solution or we find one.' KLM has its 'KLM is constante kwaliteit' (KICK) programme.

A strategy does not come alive until the units in an organization recognize it. A strategy can be initiated top-down, but it must be validated and elaborated bottom-up. This is in effect more difficult than drawing up an overall strategy. One can speak of a sound strategic plan only when each unit has specified its own responsibilities within the complete plan, and has drawn up its own action plan to realize it.

Structure

What kind of structure combines self-interest with organizational interest? Which interventions and characteristics can bring both impulses into line? An outline of the main structural characteristics of an organization is presented here.

I strongly recommend that units be made autonomous, in such a way that they can respond quickly to the (internal) market. An organization should preferably be structured in units that run distinct product categories, units with their own profit responsibility; these units should be as self-supporting as possible. Unit management should have the major authority regarding its own unit structure, market strategy and product development. Units should also have their own staff facilities.

For example, in a chemical company there was rivalry between research and development, marketing and technology. Its effects were stereotyping, fruitless bickering and sub-optimization. These functional departments were recently regrouped into product groups. The product groups were made responsible for their results; they had to come up with business plans specifying how they would improve their results. Twice a year the product groups were audited by top management. After a difficult start-up phase, relations in the product groups clearly improved. More and more people started identifying with their product groups. The former rivalry between functions was replaced to a certain extent by a mild competition among the product groups through trying to distinguish themselves by showing better results.

Organizational units can be made more self-supporting by given them control over a large part of their earnings – for example, by assigning units a fixed percentage of their gross profits. Other possible incentives would be allowing units a bonus in relation to results, developing transfer pricing arrangements based on market prices, and permitting units to buy externally if they can obtain better quality for less money. In a large company, many internal customers complained about the maintenance department: it was too slow, too expensive, and lacked service. The board was inclined to give the units more freedom to find external suppliers. This was the signal for the maintenance department to develop a more customer-oriented attitude. One important method was to arrange meetings with small groups of internal customers regularly. In the past, bottlenecks and suggestions presented by internal customers were disposed of as being 'the same old stories' and 'easy for them to say'. Now, instead of these avoiding and defensive reactions, the maintenance department has learned to regard complaints and suggestions as hard facts, which must be dealt with to the customer's satisfaction.

Such autonomy needs to be balanced with closer interdependency. One way to achieve this would be to develop a system of horizontal job rotation such as that applied in Japan. This system helps managers develop a more generalist outlook. It makes the network of dependencies more manifest and minimizes rivalries, because rivalry becomes self-defeating if a person has a chance to become one of the 'competition' himself. Management rotation is particularly important in staff departments. Too often one comes across little empires of managers who have made themselves invincible in their own field; the consolidation of their own positions has outweighed the need to cooperate.

Here are some other ways to strengthen the organization as a whole:

- Centralized career planning, backed up by central personnel facilities for recreation, housing, pension provisions, health care, study and training, and so forth.

- Central facilities that sub-units would never be able to afford, in areas such as research and development, automated systems, venture capital and availability of highly qualified managers.

- A management at arm's length which keeps a strategic course and absorbs and reconciles differences of opinion between units. If necessary it can cut the knot to prevent unproductive tussles. This central management also strives for balanced relations between units.

For example, a few years ago a software house began a process of decentralization. A more customer-oriented attitude necessitated a more flexible organization composed of relatively autonomous units. The central staff has gradually been reduced, with many people being transferred to regional offices. Only what central and regional management feel is absolutely necessary remains centralized. This has created a problem with the coordination and exchange of innovations and product developments. To support this, well-prepared workshops are held periodically. It is interesting to note that all units receive a monthly survey of the results obtained per unit for that month.

Culture

In addition to more structural interventions, a particular culture can be developed and encouraged deliberately. The culture we want is characterized by unit prominence as well as by strong common ties. Jewel Companies Inc., a retailing company with stores all over the United States, speaks very emphatically of its 'interdependent company: it is a right but also an obligation to make use of one another's knowledge.' In this context Albert Heijn, director of the largest food retailer in Holland, remarks:

> The divisions, the subsidiaries are self-supporting. You can't force the director of one division to consult another division. If, however, he consistently refuses to do so, it will be recorded in his personal record . . . Our policy is: subsidiaries can overlap, they are free to cultivate their own markets, to stimulate each other and to compete with each other.

Another original example of such a both/and culture can be found at Minnesota Mining and Manufacturing Company. Here a special place is reserved where at the end of each day everyone deposits a file showing the research he or she is working on. Others can thumb through it, make comments and give advice. This combines both of the impulses mentioned above: people are encouraged to distinguish themselves by working on something inspiring, and they can simultaneously participate in a climate of joint support, exchange and stimulation.

There are other ways to stimulate such a culture. One important factor is to encourage experimentation and internal entrepreneurship; this gives employees and units ample opportunity to work out promising ideas. In a large garage the customers frequently complained about the quality of the repairs. As a result, the internal communication – by means of work sheets and without direct customer contact – was arranged differently. When customers brought in their cars in the morning and presented their questions and complaints, the mechanic concerned was called in whenever possible. This produced an immediate improvement in results.

In addition, such a culture is stimulated by a strong emphasis on the development and profiling of the talents of the employees – in other words, an active training policy. In general, people are free to work at their own discretion. Non-conformity is even encouraged. The 'skunks' and 'skunkworks' that are advocated by Peters and Austin (1985) to facilitate innovation illustrate this well. Skunks are talented but headstrong employees who are necessary for innovation. Sensible managers leave such nuisances free to set up skunkworks – groups of people who work on highly promising projects. Presenting an almost endless number of examples, Peters and Austin demonstrate how headstrong troublemakers are of vital importance to various companies. They also show that it is not enough to encourage people to distinguish themselves by trying something new. The other side of the balance is that the organization must also form a strong safety net to catch those who fall. People take risks more readily when they know they will be well supported in the final analysis. Indeed, this is a clear example of strengthening both autonomous drive and joint solidarity! It is through impulses such as this that the organization develops an innovative climate, which increases its capability as a whole to meet challenges in the environment.

There are other possibilities for influencing the balance of tension between interdependency and autonomy. One can attempt direct intervention through the development of certain skills and a particular attitude. A clear example is influencing management style in the direction of 'management by walking around' (also known as 'management by wandering around'). In this approach, managers spend a lot of time with their employees. They facilitate communication in various ways. They strive for informal and personal relations; they are not averse to after-hours activities. They show that they can be approached. All sorts of formal distinctions and privileges (for example, separate canteens) are abolished. They invite suggestions and ideas; they elicit reactions to their own ideas. In other words, there is a systematic effort to improve the quality of communication in hierarchical relations.

Very important also is the deliberate development of teams and working relations between units. Training in problem solving, meeting methods and constructive negotiating skills is important. Building trust and more open and direct interaction in teams can become important assets in improving the quality of communication.

Information

The main problem in information management is selection: that is, how to condense the available information into a few figures that offer a true informational handle to management and employees. Ideally, each unit and organizational level should have a limited number of indicators that would periodically make visible the results obtained. Measuring results in this way provides a constant incentive for improving performance. It mobilizes energy: units know what they stand for. Chapter 8 describes many examples of this type of performance indicator.

Making results visible, and relating them to units by means of short-cycle feedback and horizontal exchange, to a certain extent replaces hierarchical steering and control. The market is drawn into the organization; each unit shows results of its own, and this mobilizes energy. The rivalry with competitors is the external impulse; the rivalry for doing well in comparison with other units is the internal impulse. Relatively small and autonomous units influence one another much more effectively than management ever could. When units have to report to higher echelons, they are more likely to adopt a defensive attitude, making statements such as 'things are different here'. The more hierarchical direction and control there is, the stronger is this tendency. It is much more effective to let the facts of the market speak for themselves.

This means that visible results must be combined with *learning*. In my view, this is one of the most promising ways of gaining from the information collected. Learning takes place at different levels: first, units hold internal consultation about the results obtained, particularly about ways of improving them; and secondly, similar units in the organization (for example, branches of the same company) compare results. This process is then combined with the exchange of ideas and experiences. Such interaction calls for good interpersonal relations; the quality of communication often becomes one of the major elements of a project to improve results.

A publishing company had recently been through an internal reorganization into market-oriented profit centres, that is groups of publishers who together cover a certain market, such as sports and recreation, culture, economy and finance. The groups were made responsible for all types of publication in their field. In the past, the organization had been much less clear-cut. The emphasis had been on product-oriented units, each with a particular type of publication: some concentrated on periodicals, others on books, others on looseleaf editions. The new units were given monthly information on indicators that were important to them, such as costs and turnovers. To strengthen the position of the company, management had to face the difficult problem of developing the entrepreneurship of the units: 'How can we encourage the entrepreneur in the company?' To bring this into practice, management set down a few important conditions in the form of questions:

- To what extent do units learn from one another's successes and failures?
- Do the units exhibit enough horizontal exchange and support to strengthen tendencies to success?
- Does the monthly information give a realistic picture of success and failure tendencies?
- How might this information be used to ensure that the maximum benefit is drawn from it?
- To what extent are there rewards for outstanding results?
- Are there enough opportunities for initiatives and experiments?

In several workshops the conditions were converted into practical guidelines with the help of those directly involved. Management then worked at putting them into practice. These impulses helped to implement an increasingly successful internal entrepreneurship.

THE ORGANIZATIONAL MODEL

We have explained how the balance of autonomy and interdependency can be influenced in such a way that it yields a productive tension in organizations. Strategy, structure, culture and information management all provide opportunities for realizing an optimal tension balance. In essence it concerns managing interdependencies within and between units in the direction of creating a separate store for each unit, and at the same time stressing 'let's do it together.'

Figure 2.2[2] summarizes our major conclusions up to this point.

[2] There are many organizational models of this type, for instance the 7-S model by Peters and Waterman (1982). The key question concerns the way in which the separate elements are linked. This question is nearly always neglected. Authors design boxes with arrows and connecting lines; what these arrows and lines stand for remains unclear. They suggest specific relationships and influences; however, the what and how are nearly always implicit. We need more explicit relations between aspects. In practice we even need a way of designing organizations in which aspects are consistent with each other, mutually supportive and reinforcing. In our view, different aspects fit into the autonomy–interdependency model as an integrative perspective, which also shows how elements can be designed in a coherent supportive and reinforcing way.

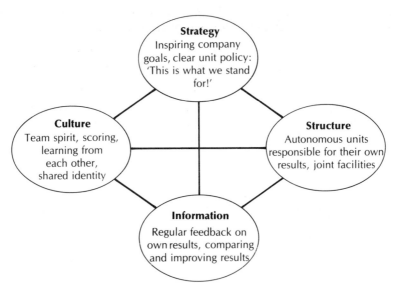

FIGURE 2.2 Incentives for motivation

All in all we are dealing with a sophisticated organization here. It is particularly interesting that hierarchical direction and control are partially replaced by horizontal exchange and comparison. Unit results are made more visible and are reported back more quickly. This mobilizes energy.

Developmental framework

The proper management of interdependencies within and between organizations is becoming a fundamentally critical factor for success. Organizations are increasingly becoming relatively flat *configurations of negotiating relations*. Units are autonomous, while cultivating simultaneously those interdependencies that give them a competitive edge.

This gives a different substance to the relationship of centralized to decentralized. The swing of the pendulum from central to decentral becomes a dynamic tension balance of both central *and* decentral.

The characteristics of the central organization are:

- Specification of the strategy (an inspiring statement of the core business and common values).

- Development of the organization in the direction of units that are responsible for their performance.

- Stimulation and facilitation of units to make their own results visible and to work systematically on improving performance.

- Attention to the quality of communication, for example by ensuring a good horizontal exchange of results and ideas to improve performance.

- More focus on the process of continually improving performance rather than on the contents; the fact that people work at improvement is more important than the operational improvement itself.

- Selection and strengthening of critical interdependencies, for example the company formula, management development and financial systems.

In the decentralized framework:

- Units formulate their own output indicators within the policy framework.

- Units set up their own plans to improve results.

- There is a high degree of unit autonomy to determine what means will be employed in what ways to achieve better results.

- Units are free to profile themselves according to their own style and identity.

- Units have sufficient resources to achieve their own plans; there is little dependency on central departments.

- Supporting services are farmed out; there is a market relationship with the remaining central services.

Networks of negotiating relations

The concept of the pyramid is no longer suited to the service organization; rather, it is a network of units that are free to act while retaining their links with one another. The direction in which the network moves and the quality of relations within it are shaped by the more central units, but the units also show responsibility for these functions. In particular, horizontal exchange and coordination demand that every unit is an active network member. This theme is repeated within units. Teams are effective only if they know they are responsible for the organizational unit; individuals can be prominent only if they feel a responsibility for the team of which they are a part.

These processes demand certain social skills of the participants: initiative and an eagerness to show results, combined with the activation of flexible horizontal relations in which integrative potential is developed and new combinations can be formed. The ability to negotiate constructively and creatively and to function well in teams is indispensable for this.

In its most advanced form, we see the both/and nature of relations in such a horizontal network expressed at each intersection. There is a feeling of responsibility for the unit as well as for the larger whole of which it is a part. Each unit focuses on improving its own results, but it is also a microcosm of the totality and can help compensate where capacities are lacking. In short, units help one another to function better.

This type of organization is on the rise because it can better deal with competition. The most important reasons for this are the reduction of complexity and bureaucracy, and the mobilization of a high energy. By experimenting, mostly by trial and error, this kind of organization is becoming a reality. We are going through a transition to a higher integration level, one that is equipped for more complexity!

For example, consider two entirely different organizations, both of which have developed in this direction. The first is BSO, a software development firm in The Netherlands. Its formula is based on the principle of cell division. Units have a limit of 65 employees; if they grow beyond that number, they are split up. The units are independent companies with responsibility for their own sales, recruitment, personnel policy, purchasing and investments: only financial systems and part of research and development are centralized staff services. This firm is one of the fastest growing software houses in The Netherlands.

The second is the Westland Flower Auction, one of a number of cooperatives in The Netherlands which have traditionally followed a pattern that is increasingly evolving in the direction described. The Westland Flower Auction consists of 2500 autonomous entrepreneurs; these entrepreneurs have considerably strengthened their position through their concerted efforts on the client market. Furthermore, the Westland Flower Auction is in a position to mobilize all kinds of expertise and information to which completely autonomous companies would have less direct access. This type of configuration has proven to be a great competitive power on the world market. The cooperative flower auctions in The Netherlands handle 60 per cent of the world trade in flowers.

These are two very different variations on the same basic pattern. It is typical that, even though the two formulas are reasonably crystallized, the balance of autonomy and interdependency remains in motion. Ongoing discussions, doubts and adjustments ensure that the autonomy–interdependency balance develops as a dynamic entity, adapting to the business environment.

CONCLUSIONS

Customer orientation and quality demand a high level of dedication and motivation. How can this be achieved? The points of action in this context are the interdependencies between and within organizational units. The goal is the realization of a productive tension between units. Both autonomy and interdependency must be developed; some incentives to this end are shown in table 2.1.

TABLE 2.1 The tension balance between autonomy and interdependency: examples of incentives

Autonomy	Interdependency
Profit centres with large degree of autonomy concerning internal structure, investments, product development and market strategy	Company facilities in areas such as research, financing risks, management development and rare expertise
Flatter organization	Horizontal mobility
Encourage initiative/experiments	Safety net for setbacks
Team spirit, management by walking around	Clear mission, sense of belonging, house style, informal relations
Constant feedback and comparison of results per unit	Increase of mutual effectiveness by learning from and teaching each other
We vs the 'internal competitor'	We vs the external competitor

It is especially important that units achieve short and direct lines to the market. The market is drawn into the organization. Everyone is aware of (internal) customers and results. Comparison with the results of others is a strong incentive; so is the mutual exchange of experiences.[3]

[3] Are these principles equally valid for the non-profit sector? The core elements of the intended approach can be summarized in four questions:

• How clearly can customers and clients be designated?
• How clear are their questions?
• How clear are the delivered products?
• How clear are the results?

The management of interdependencies demands a certain tolerance, or even fostering, of opposing forces. It is concerned with the realization of a tension balance, a dynamic balance of both centripetal *and* centrifugal forces. This constitutes a lever for energy and vitality. We have summarized this development by means of four concepts:

Strategy Concise formulating of the core activities, the company goals and the desired type of organization (management philosophy, style of interaction, external image); clear unit policy.

Structure Units have their own (internal) customers and products, combined with responsibilities and the means to really influence their own results.

Culture High-quality communication within and between units, close-knit teams, informal relations.

Information Visible results for all units, access to results of the whole, short-cycle feedback.

Another way of expressing more closely the heart of this development is the following. *Within* units, a strong sense of interdependency develops. The manifest need to compete and to do well on the (internal) market stimulates internal solidarity, motivation and entrepreneurship. *Between* units, a productive tension emerges which is partly generated by exchanging results. The interdependency is simultaneously enhanced by interventions such as horizontal mobility, shared goals and shared identity, frequent informal contacts and exchanges throughout the entire organization.

These questions are simple but sometimes hard to answer. The more a non-profit organization is geared up to giving clear answers to these questions, the easier it becomes to generate the positive dynamics described above. This is especially so if there is a structure of units which have integral responsibility for a specific market of customers and/or target groups – and even more so if exchange and comparison with other units are possible.

These four questions can also be regarded as four auditing criteria which provide a picture of the added value of an organizational unit. Rendering this added value visible is sometimes complicated by the lack of market signals. This is not an insurmountable problem. There are alternatives for price and market share signals: the profit principle, opinion and satisfaction measurement, client panels, complaint analysis, shadow prices, panels of opinion leaders and output measurement. Developing a feedback system is essential. It is an alternative for market signals.

REFERENCES

Mastenbroek, W.F.G. 1987: *Conflict Management and Organization Development.* Chichester, New York: Wiley.

Peters, T.J. and Austin, N. 1985: *A Passion for Excellence.* New York: Random House.

Peters, T.J. and Waterman, R.H. 1982: *In Search of Excellence.* New York: Harper and Row.

PART II

Supporting models and techniques

3

Organizational conditions and motivation: a diagnostic instrument

WILLEM F.G. MASTENBROEK

INTRODUCTION

Greater quality, more service, more flexibility, cost awareness, innovative capacity: these have become the battle-cries. Programmes and instruments are made available to promote all this. These tools can offer real help, but soon it becomes clear that commitment and motivation are critical factors.

Motivation cannot be developed by a quick fix. It is related to organizational conditions. In chapter 2 we examined conditions and incentives from the perspectives of strategy, structure, culture and information (figure 3.1). The questionnaire in this chapter describes 28 possibilities stemming from those perspectives. It enables a management team to

FIGURE 3.1 Four perspectives for looking at motivation

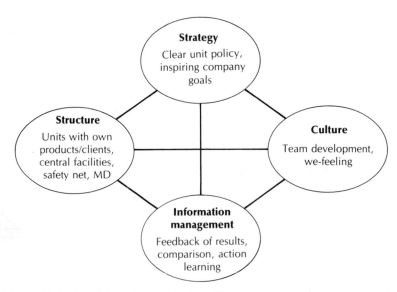

FIGURE 3.2 Conditions for motivation (1)

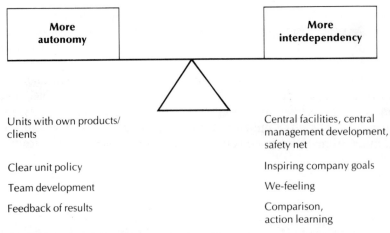

FIGURE 3.3 Conditions for motivation (2)

make up its mind about the most promising leverage points. It can also be used to learn how units in the organization experience their situation, and what suggestions they have in mind.

Another concept is the autonomy–interdependency balance: integrate your company by decentralization! This concept is elaborated briefly in chapter 2 and more extensively in Mastenbroek (1987). In my experience it proves to be a fruitful approach for understanding the basic driving forces of motivation. Moreover, this concept enables us to see a pattern in seemingly disparate changes. This is important because, in a motivating organization, concrete actions and interventions need to fit into an overall vision. The questionnaire is built around the autonomy–interdependency concept. Figures 3.2 and 3.3 summarize these ideas.

QUESTIONNAIRE: CONDITIONS FOR MOTIVATION IN YOUR ORGANIZATION

This instrument has been designed to indicate how your organization is balancing autonomy and interdependency. This balance is a key factor in determining the motivation and commitment of individual organizational members. It is also directly related to the common purpose and identity of the organization as a whole. The instrument provides clues about the opportunities in your organization to raise motivation.

The questions refer to your work situation, and have been designed to elicit your opinions. There are therefore no such things as right or wrong answers. Your responses will be treated confidentially. Please answer the questions as frankly as possible.

You are requested to respond to each question twice: first for the *current* situation, and then for the *desired* situation.

	Not at all	To a small degree	Some-where in between	Reasonable	To a high degree
1 Improvements and renewal are stimulated in our department.					
NOW	1	2	3	4	5
DESIRED	1	2	3	4	5
2 We have clearly defined areas of responsibility in our department (own clients/products/markets).					
NOW	1	2	3	4	5
DESIRED	1	2	3	4	5

continued

	Not at all	To a small degree	Some- where in between	Reasonable	To a high degree
3 I know how our customers regard the products and/or services of our department.					
NOW	1	2	3	4	5
DESIRED	1	2	3	4	5
4 I am aware of the costs of the different products/services of our department.					
NOW	1	2	3	4	5
DESIRED	1	2	3	4	5
5 Departments in our organization have highly motivating objectives.					
NOW	1	2	3	4	5
DESIRED	1	2	3	4	5
6 When an important job vacancy occurs a suitable candidate is sought within our own organization.					
NOW	1	2	3	4	5
DESIRED	1	2	3	4	5
7 This organization stimulates horizontal job rotation.					
NOW	1	2	3	4	5
DESIRED	1	2	3	4	5
8 Our department has its own budget.					
NOW	1	2	3	4	5
DESIRED	1	2	3	4	5

	Not at all	To a small degree	Some- where in between	Reasonable	To a high degree
9 There is a strong relationship between rewards and achievement in this organization.					
NOW	1	2	3	4	5
DESIRED	1	2	3	4	5
10 When our department is 'up against it' it can count on support from the rest of the organization.					
NOW	1	2	3	4	5
DESIRED	1	2	3	4	5
11 Ideas and initiatives from our department are taken seriously in the rest of the organization.					
NOW	1	2	3	4	5
DESIRED	1	2	3	4	5
12 Communication between our department and higher organizational levels and central departments is good.					
NOW	1	2	3	4	5
DESIRED	1	2	3	4	5
13 People in our department feel personally responsible for the results of their work.					
NOW	1	2	3	4	5
DESIRED	1	2	3	4	5

continued

	Not at all	To a small degree	Some- where in between	Reasonable	To a high degree
14 Departments in our organization learn from each other's experiences.					
NOW	1	2	3	4	5
DESIRED	1	2	3	4	5
15 The results of our department are made visible to us from time to time.					
NOW	1	2	3	4	5
DESIRED	1	2	3	4	5
16 We have the information to compare the results of our department with those of other departments.					
NOW	1	2	3	4	5
DESIRED	1	2	3	4	5
17 Everyone who works here knows what the organization as a whole stands for.					
NOW	1	2	3	4	5
DESIRED	1	2	3	4	5
18 Senior management of this organization checks our views before determining important matters of policy.					
NOW	1	2	3	4	5
DESIRED	1	2	3	4	5

	Not at all	To a small degree	Some-where in between	Reasonable	To a high degree
19 My supervisor is interested in my ideas.					
NOW	1	2	3	4	5
DESIRED	1	2	3	4	5
20 This organization has inspiring objectives.					
NOW	1	2	3	4	5
DESIRED	1	2	3	4	5
21 I get stimulating suggestions about my work from my colleagues in my department.					
NOW	1	2	3	4	5
DESIRED	1	2	3	4	5
22 We know how our organization is doing compared with other similar organizations.					
NOW	1	2	3	4	5
DESIRED	1	2	3	4	5
23 Our entire organization is focused on 'doing it better' than other similar organizations.					
NOW	1	2	3	4	5
DESIRED	1	2	3	4	5
24 There is an informal, cooperative climate in our department.					
NOW	1	2	3	4	5
DESIRED	1	2	3	4	5

continued

	Not at all	To a small degree	Some-where in between	Reasonable	To a high degree
25 The different departments within this organization cooperate effectively.					
NOW	1	2	3	4	5
DESIRED	1	2	3	4	5
26 Senior management is aware of the problems experienced within the organization.					
NOW	1	2	3	4	5
DESIRED	1	2	3	4	5
27 I personally subscribe to our department's policies and objectives.					
NOW	1	2	3	4	5
DESIRED	1	2	3	4	5
28 This organization does a great deal for its members.					
NOW	1	2	3	4	5
DESIRED	1	2	3	4	5

Now that you have completed the questionnaire, do you have any additional remarks or comments? You may write these down in the space below.

Many thanks for your cooperation!

Now proceed to the scoring form and profile.

SCORING FOR AUTONOMY AND INTERDEPENDENCY

Please enter your responses in the following table.

Autonomy   **Interdependency**

Question	Now	Desired	Absolute difference	Question	Now	Desired	Absolute difference
1				6			
2				7			
3				10			
4				11			
5				12			
8				14			
9				17			
13				18			
15				20			
16				22			
19				23			
21				25			
24				26			
27				28			

Totals

continued

You may now enter your totals on the following scoring profile. The higher you score on autonomy and interdependency, the greater the chance that high levels of dedication and motivation are characteristic of your department and your organization.

	Autonomy		Interdependency	
	NOW	DESIRED	NOW	DESIRED
70				
60				
50				
40				
30				
20				
10				

Leverage Points for Change

For which questions is the difference between current and desired situations the greatest?

-
-
-

Do you see any opportunities to do something about these areas? If so, formulate a few concrete action steps.

-
-
-

REFERENCE

Mastenbroek, W.F.G. 1987: *Conflict Management and Organization Development.* Chichester, New York: Wiley.

4

The quality quadrant: which quality problems do we tackle first?

GERCO C. EZERMAN

INTRODUCTION

An organization starts up a project of systematic quality improvement. A steering committee is installed, which prepares a management conference. At this conference the final decision is made to carry out the project, and it is also decided that the start will consist of a meeting for all employees. Top management itself will get on the soapbox to motivate everybody. At the meeting, the introductions emphasize concrete aspects of quality improvement: everyone must answer letters within two weeks, and accessibility by telephone must be improved considerably. Those present react with scepticism (after the meeting). Why aren't the real problems tackled? Each person can point out several of these problems: the style of management, the rickety approach to automation, the lack of clear policy.

A second organization, a transport company, also starts a quality project. The central issue is improving the quality of service to the passengers. An information film is shown to clarify (with considerable humour) everything the passengers suffer. A market research firm is called in to examine why the public decides in favour of or against the transportation package offered, and how it evaluates the package. The film and research results are discussed extensively in management conferences. Motivating the departments towards concrete quality actions turns out to be very difficult. Eighteen months after the starting conferences, the board confesses that this approach did not work. Perhaps there was too much of an outward orientation, causing the burden of the quality project to fall largely on the drivers and ticket collectors. However, how can a driver be expected to be more service oriented if he is not served well by his own technical department?

In a large hospital the technical department, whose main tasks are building projects and maintenance, also wants to improve its performance. In a one and a half day meeting with executives, it examines which issues should be improved. The main emphasis is on the complexity of the internal coordination and communication structure, and the lack of effective cooperation between various disciplines. After the conference, working groups set out to indicate solutions for the various problems. A large number of solutions is presented, but six months after the conference the head of the department announces that he sees little in the proposed improvements. It has all been tried before; he has little confidence that the internal discipline exists to actually implement and stabilize the improvements. The course of the improvement process so far has, however, strengthened his conviction that the real problems have remained untouched. He and several members of his staff define the real problems as uncertainty about the continued existence of the current tasks and size of the department. Shouldn't we expand into the external market? Wouldn't it be better to privatize various maintenance tasks?

FOUR AREAS OF QUALITY IMPROVEMENT

What do these three examples of the practice of faltering quality improvement processes have in common? In each of the organizations, management is strongly motivated for quality improvement. It does not decide to cancel the project after the first (not very successful) steps in the improvement process, but instead searches for improvements in approach. Furthermore, the examples share to some degree the project approach, with steering committees, working groups, quality plans etc. A third characteristic is that all three examples involve the entire (higher and middle) management in the project, and the first two include the employees. And a fourth characteristic of the three examples is that first a certain type of quality problem is selected, and subsequently this choice is subjected to discussion once again! How can we describe these types of quality problem?

Two main questions form the basis for the initial selection of the quality problems. The first question is: do we aim to improve service to the external customer (the public, the passengers), or do we focus on the quality of internal cooperation (in the third example)? In other words: is the central issue one of *external* or *internal* quality? Deciding in favour of external quality will undeniably open up a discussion concerning whether the front line employees are effectively supplied with their tools by internally oriented departments, management included. If the decision is in favour of internal quality, strategic questions such as 'Who are our external customers, now and in the future?' cannot be ignored.

The second main question is: do we tackle *small* or *large* quality problems? Small quality problems are caused by failure to observe standards in everyday work, perhaps through ignorance of those standards. Large quality problems refer to the poor supply of requested services and products. For example, a small quality improvement might be that everyone answers the phone within three rings. A large quality improvement in that case would be to install a telecommunications system with follow-me characteristics, i.e. a new internal service product. Small quality can also be defined as *service* quality; correspondingly, large quality refers to the specification of products and services, i.e. *product* quality.

Both dimensions – internal/external and small/large – can be brought together in the quality quadrant shown in figure 4.1. This quadrant was developed by the author within the framework of a research project regarding the nature and size of quality improvement actions in Dutch

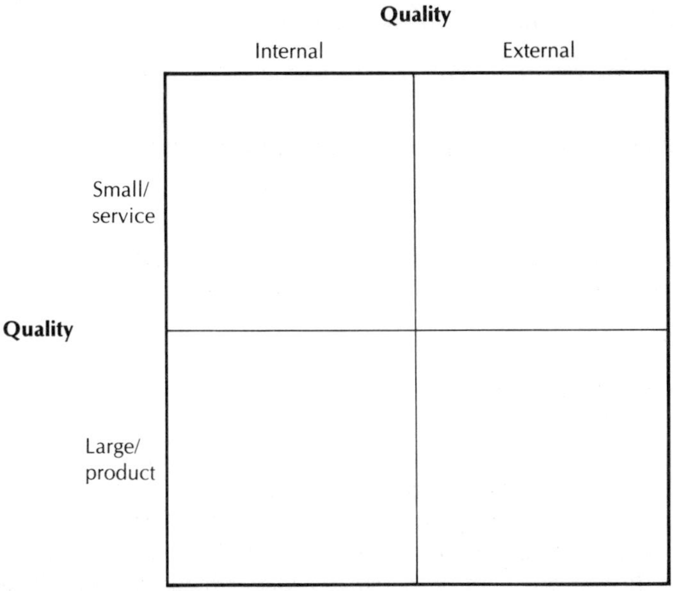

FIGURE 4.1 The quality quadrant

government organizations. The quadrant enables classification of the various projects. Subsequently it has been used frequently in all kinds of workshops at the start of various quality programmes.

USING THE QUALITY QUADRANT

The quadrant can be very helpful during workshops in categorizing the problems with which the quality project could concern itself. It commands a broad inventory, avoiding the one-sidedness described in the three cases earlier. This section outlines the typical quality problems that can emerge in such an inventory.

Small internal

- Opening times, duration of meetings
- Internal communication
- Preparing meetings
- Atmosphere
- Accessibility, availability of management
- Mistakes in internal written correspondence (for example salary records)
- Clarity of the information of financial departments
- Neatness, hygiene.

The goal of small internal activity is to dot the *i*s and cross the *t*s, to improve internal discipline and internal working relations.

Large internal

The large internal class refers to improving the quality of services and products supplied by one organizational department to another. In other words, the aim is to clarify the specifications of internal products and to gather information for the realization of these specifications. For example, the products of a personnel department are social annual reports, training plans, training programmes, recruiting and selection procedures, statutes of reorganization and reviews of personnel data. Specifications of these products might be:

- Timely delivery
- Involvement of internal customers in production
- Budgets
- Production times
- Intended results
- Intelligibility.

Improving large internal quality therefore means providing the various internal products with quantitative specifications or norms. Then the feasibility of these specifications is assessed.

Small external

Here the relationship with the external customer is the central issue. Typical characteristics include:

- Nature, number, costs of complaints
- Queuing at cash desks, counters
- Waiting periods (in hospitals, etc.)
- Nature and number of noes (in a retail company)
- Accessibility by telephone
- Clarity of internal signposting
- Atmosphere in contacts with customers (the McDonalds smile)
- Recording customer information.

Large external

This resembles the large internal category, but this time in dealings with external customers.

Table 4.1 shows typical major product and service specifications.

TABLE 4.1

Major product specifications	*Major service specifications*
Delivery time	Access time
Fitness for use	Waiting periods
Duration of production process	Manageability
Involvement of customers	Atmosphere
Budget	Ability to identify with customer
Maintenance sensitivity	Handling complaints
Introduction	Physical appearance

DETERMINING PRIORITIES

Which of the quality problems emerging from the inventory deserves priority? Obviously it is impossible to tackle everything at once. In this context, two different opinions can be heard. The first is: let's tackle the internal quality first. It is more easily mastered, and in addition this will automatically lead to improvements in external quality. The second opinion is: start with external quality. This will improve relations with our sponsors, on whom we are dependent in the end. Besides, if we focus exclusively on internal quality, we run the risk of expending our energy on matters which have no relevance for the external customer.

Which of these opinions is correct? In my experience, working on internal quality is by no means simpler than working on external quality. For example, I observe time and time again the difficulties in getting internal customer surveys off the ground – or the effort it takes to get management to regard the employees as customers who can be asked to provide specifications of management services.

On the other hand, working on external quality is equally difficult for some organizations. Take for example a directorate in a ministry, where the following question arises: who *are* our customers? Are they just the ministers, or do they include other departments, or even executive institutions such as inspectorates, or the general public?

Based on our experiences in various quality programmes, we recommend consideration of the following items when trying to decide which quality problems to tackle:

1 The ideal situation would be that every department in an organization starts working on quality. For some departments this will

mean external quality, for others internal quality (staff departments).

2 On the other hand, it is often very difficult to command a total quality programme as described under 1. Therefore: start your programme where sufficient support is guaranteed. In the case of a certain university this meant that the internal services and one or two faculties started working on internal and external quality improvement respectively.

3 We recommend in all cases that top management (in cooperation with higher and middle management) develops a quality policy in which all four quality fields are addressed. Which departments in the organization will start on concrete quality programmes then depends on the following factors:

(a) Is continuity of the department's management guaranteed?

(b) Is the department not already engaged in a process of reorganization?

(c) Can the department, in view of other change processes, generate sufficient attention for a specific quality action?

(d) Are management and employees truly motivated for a programme?

4 If the answers to the questions posed under 3 are affirmative regarding a specific department in the organization, then this department can start implementing the quality policy. An important starting activity is to make an inventory of quality problems with the aid of the quality quadrant described above. This is a joint activity for management and employees.

5 At departmental level the question now arises: which of the problems listed do we tackle first? An important role in selecting the problem is reserved for the (internal or external) customers. Market research or internal perception evaluation are accepted methods. In addition, interviewing a sample of major customers can yield other quality problems. Working on quality always entails setting up suitable communication with the customers. This communication can take place by means of interviews, questionnaires, observation of customers, complaint analysis and image research (table 4.2).

6 Alternative perspectives for selecting the quality problems to be tackled:

(a) Can we render the problem visible and measurable?

(b) Can we as a department solve the problem ourselves?

These questions refer to the degree in which the quality problems can be controlled.

TABLE 4.2 Methods of collecting customer information

Questionnaires (written); market research; internal perception evaluation

Registration of 'prouds and sorries'; complaint systems

Workshops with customers; panel discussions

Observation of customer behaviour: waiting periods, queuing, having to say 'no' etc.

Recording communication (tape, video)

Observation of product specification (checklists)

CONCLUSIONS

The key question in this chapter was: which quality problems do we tackle? Two principal notions were discussed. The first was that we recommend a broad inventory of quality problems; here the quality quadrant can be used as an aid. The second was that management and employees cooperate in this inventory and in determining priorities, and that customers are also involved.

Working on quality improvement in this manner, provided it is done correctly, is a stimulating experience for all concerned.

5

Diagnosis of quality in service: the quality scales in auditing customer–supplier relations

LEO A.F. M. KERKLAAN

INTRODUCTION

Quality programmes are initiated by service organizations when they are confronted with strongly increasing competitive pressure from outside. It is not until clients react vehemently that quality and innovation are (re)born. The management of these service organizations is suddenly faced with the question: 'What does quality actually mean to us?'

Eventually the decision is made to really start working on quality. This is often done in the form of a 'quality in top' or 'quality is key' programme. The total service process is considered fully. In search of fitness for use for both external and internal customers, product specifications are determined again for every link in the chain of production. In the process, internal customer orientation also becomes an important theme.

Deviations from product specifications are defects. However, we can learn from them. Mistakes become visible in the contacts between customers and their suppliers. A quality programme needs an instrument that can help identify and assess the interfaces in the organization. The instrument should be relatively simple and recognizable in all kinds of business situations.

Here we present the so-called quality scales. With this instrument one can rapidly form an impression of whether the relation between the customer and the supplier is a healthy one. In a more detailed form this instrument is used as an audit. With the aid of a number of basic questions it is possible to assess the customer–supplier relationship at a particular interface.

First we address at greater length the concepts of customer orientation and quality. We go on to discuss the possibility of giving objective evidence of process quality using interfaces. Then we discuss the principle on which our main instrument, the quality scales, is based. Next we describe three equilibrium situations which can be distinguished with the scales. Finally we consider the practical application of the scales, with special focus on their use as an audit instrument. Eighteen measuring questions are presented, which provide a complete picture of the quality situation at a certain interface.

CUSTOMER ORIENTATION

Quality is determined exclusively by the external customer's satisfaction

A strong customer orientation characterizes the service industry. In former times, this positive trait frequently resulted in the service industry not having its own business under control – which is not surprising.

In small-scale service industry it was often possible to solve quality problems by improvising. Therefore the discussion about quality primarily referred to the quality of service as finally experienced by the customer. And rightly so, because only the external customer's satisfaction determines the quality of the services provided (figure 5.1).

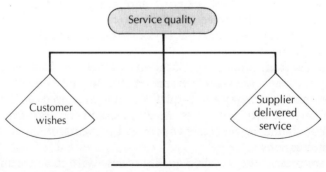

FIGURE 5.1 Determining service quality

Balance as an indicator of quality

In this view, quality is right when the scales are in balance; that is, balance is a prerequisite for top quality. However, the balance should be based on sufficient elements. Otherwise one cannot speak of real quality – the complete satisfaction of an external customer.

Here we run up against a problem: quality is a diffuse notion, hard to grasp. Nobody is against quality, but we all have a different notion of it. For one person it is zero defects in the end result; for another it means a long life span of the product. It is an illusion to think that answers such as these can lead to clarity. For when do we speak of a defect? And what is a long life span? Generally speaking, a packet of peppermints does not last as long as an electric bulb. However, a manufacturing error may be of much more importance in a bulb than in a peppermint.

Quality from the customer's perspective

From these examples it becomes clear that the (final) customer plays a key role in defining quality. For instance, it is nonsense to set the tolerance of peppermints at 0.01 mm; the consumer wouldn't notice a difference of 0.1 mm. In producing peppermints it is much more important to aim at constant taste and composition, because these are the factors a customer notices.

When determining the quality standard of a service, the supplier should ensure that it fits the client's needs perfectly. As Dr J.M. Juran put it years ago: 'Quality is fitness for use.' The customer decides about quality.

Quality from the supplier's perspective

Nowadays, however, everybody is aware that constantly high service quality can only be attained when it is backed up by good internal organization. The process by which services are generated is essential, and it too should therefore meet a certain quality standard.

One can look at quality in two ways. From the customer's perspective, the primary focus is on the (final) quality of the end product. From the supplier's perspective the main focus is on the quality of the production process – the way in which to achieve the desired performance. That is why a true supplier of services will regularly examine his processes and reorganize them if necessary (figure 5.2).

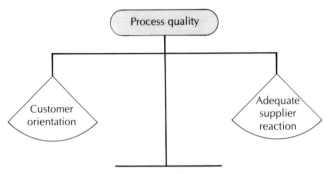

FIGURE 5.2 Determining process quality

The quality scales cannot be balanced when the supplier is insufficiently informed about the wishes of the client (insufficient orientation), or if he does not offer enough (inadequate reaction). In either case one cannot speak of fitness for intended use.

Total model for service quality

When we combine both perspectives, a total picture emerges for quality in the service industries as in figure 5.3. From this picture we can easily see that service quality depends on process quality to a large degree. We will address the issue of realizing this process quality first. To this end the process quality scales will be elaborated.

This chapter was written from the supplier's perspective, but we will not exclude the external customer. It will become clear that we can work on improving both external and internal customer orientation from the same underlying principles.

MEASURING PROCESS QUALITY

Process quality can be measured

The process of generating services always consists of several links. Every link adds something until the quality is reached that is finally offered to the customer. On the other hand, every extra link creates its own risk

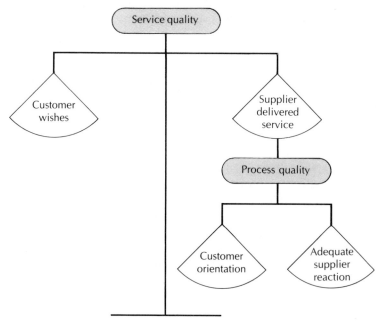

FIGURE 5.3 Total quality

of defects. In larger service organizations the number of links may easily increase to ten, making the process very complex. There is no longer anything of an old-fashioned or small-scale nature to be found. It is clear that customer orientation is at stake, and the number of defects will increase. Audit and reorganization attempt to solve this problem of insufficient feel for the customer's needs.

Because customer orientation is such a traditional value in the service industry, it is obvious that attempts will be made to extend it to the 'internal customer'. With regard to his wishes and demands, he is seen as the representative of the external client. From this perspective, the internal customer should be served equally well. An attempt is also made to ensure that the various wishes from internal customers correspond with those of the external customer. As a result of this customer orientation, an internal client–supplier relation develops between two successive links in the chain at the interface. If we want to measure (or prove) our process quality, we must measure our internal customer orientation at each interface.

Quality creation precedes quality realization

Furthermore, in its role of supplier every link has its own quality responsibility, for which it is accountable. This can occur at the interface between two different, successive activities in the chain of production. There the internal customer controls the realization of what the final customer wants. For at this point we have a tangible intermediate product. The supplying link should in fact deliver exactly what the next link (the internal client) needs to be able to continue immediately.

For this reason the supplier should thoroughly investigate the internal customer's wishes. That is the moment of quality creation. The reaction of the supplier should be such that he meets the wishes of the customer efficiently. That is to say he should provide not too little, but at the same time not too much quality. He must also watch his own interest. Quality control is no democracy. Put differently: the reaction of the supplier and the customer's wishes should be balanced. That is quality realization.

Figure 5.4 summarizes this process.

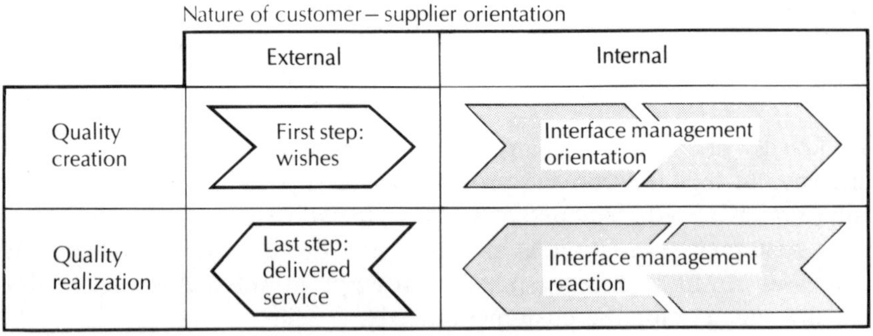

Nature of customer – supplier orientation

	External	Internal
Quality creation	First step: wishes	Interface management orientation
Quality realization	Last step: delivered service	Interface management reaction

FIGURE 5.4 The process of quality realization

The importance of extra quality

It becomes clear from figure 5.4 that the evidence of external customer orientation is mainly provided in the first and the last step. In these steps there is face-to-face contact with the customer.

Generally, services are not tangible. That is why in the first and last step we should give much attention to the environment in which the service is delivered (as well as the actual required service, of course).

This 'visiting card' determines the customer's first impression of the organization. It includes the behaviour and personal appearance of employees, and the personal relationship which is developed with the client. This is *extra quality*.

In figure 5.4 we can recognize both the perspectives from which we can look at quality. On the left side, 'on stage', we see the service quality scales again. In the wings, we are dealing with the process quality scales to which interface management is the key. For in the intermediate steps, and particularly at the interfaces between steps, internal customer orientation can be demonstrated. The supplier must prove that his service meets the fixed internal product specifications. But in this case also one can speak of quality that exceeds these fixed specifications, namely extra quality. That is what makes the difference between a colleague and a highly appreciated colleague.

THE PRINCIPLE OF THE QUALITY SCALES

Interface management depends on the internal customer–supplier relationship

Only when there is firm and adequate management at each interface can the required quality be guaranteed. The assumptions behind our instrument are that interface management is determined by the relationship between internal customer and supplier, and that the quality of the relationship can be accounted for at the interface.

What is characteristic of a healthy internal customer–supplier relationship?

The central thesis is that a healthy customer–supplier relationship is characterized by a balance between:

- Demonstrable orientation towards the internal customer (as the party who passes on the external customer's requirements)
- Adequate supplier reaction based on this orientation.

Here we clearly see that internal and external customer orientation are approached in an identical way. The trend is obvious. The supplier must react adequately and meet the wishes of the (internal and external) customer. The major difference between the external and the internal customer is that the external customer (who determines whether the quality is good) is generally in a position to change suppliers. For the internal customer this is usually impossible; the supplier determines the process quality. Therefore extra care should be taken. In fact each interface between the successive links in the production chain should be examined to establish whether a balance exists or not (figure 5.5).

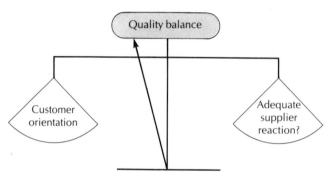

FIGURE 5.5 The quality scales

Who decides to which side the scale tips?

Here we distinguish between the two situations mentioned earlier.

Supplier not sufficiently informed or too self-centred

The scale tips to the right side in favour of the (re)actions of the supplier (figure 5.6). In this situation the supplier is insufficiently oriented towards the customer; he is contemplating his navel.

The supplier is insufficiently customer oriented if he is not able to transform customer wishes into clear agreements about the services to be delivered. There can be all kinds of reasons for this: he does not take the necessary time, or he is not really interested. Even if the internal customer does not think it is very important, it is still the supplier's task to record expectations in clear agreements and guarantees.

Instructions and procedures from the departments responsible for

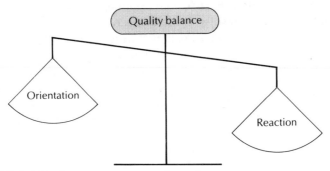

FIGURE 5.6 Inadequate customer orientation

personnel or electronic data processing, for instance, are often set up from the supplier's frame of reference. The same goes for time schedules based only on the workload capabilities of the issuing department. This of course can easily irritate the internal client.

Supplier sufficiently informed, but does not offer enough

The second possibility is that the supplier is fairly well informed about the client's needs. However, he fails to take sufficient measures to realize them, or to explain later why things didn't work out. Then the scale tips to the left side, towards customer orientation (figure 5.7). The performance is insufficient; the customer experiences it as a failure. This situation often occurs in internal customer–supplier relations. For example, a document has to be at a certain department before a certain date, without mistakes. Of course it arrives late, and furthermore con-

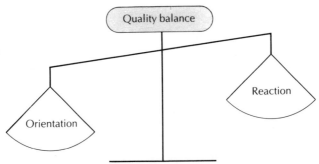

FIGURE 5.7 Inadequate supplier reaction

tains mistakes. We don't meet the expectations of the internal client in a reasonable way. This results in dissatisfaction.

There is another reason why the scale can tip to the left. It is possible that the customer makes unreasonable demands: some assignment must be finished 'by tomorrow'; or the compensation is unrealistic. It is the supplier's task to convince the customer that he cannot accept the assignment under these conditions. As we said before: quality is not a democracy. The true provider of services returns to the basic problem of what the customer wants, and he searches for a fitting solution. Consultants will recognize this situation. Clients often express unrealistic wishes at the initial contact; the presenting problem is never the real problem.

EXTENSION OF THE QUALITY SCALES: THREE BALANCE SITUATIONS

We have developed the quality scales further from the analysis above. To the notions of customer orientation and supplier reaction we have added a number of elements which help describe the balance even more precisely. We use six elements, always linked in pairs. Thus we can differentiate three balance situations to visualize the relation between customer and supplier (figure 5.8).

In order to obtain more confidence in the fact that this simple model covers reality sufficiently, we now describe it in more detail with the aid of the three balance situations. We will not distinguish between internal and external customers; from the examples and explanations it should

FIGURE 5.8 Three balance situations

be clear that the scales can chart both internal and external customer orientation.

Survey of customer expectations vs supply of products

Orientation towards external or internal customers implies orientation towards persons who have an interest in a service, or towards dependent colleagues with a similar interest.

A person who does not take into account the expectations and needs of his external or internal customers is, in fact, neither a pleasant colleague nor a good supplier of services. For this supplier does not lend a helping hand. Insufficient orientation results in providing wrong or inadequate information. The contribution of the supplier is incomplete, contains inaccuracies or is late. As emphasized above, the offer of the supplier should perfectly fit the needs of the client. Thus this balance measurement reflects the *present market potential of a supplier*.

Alternative suppliers vs positioning of supplier

As a result of quality defects, customers or colleagues are going to look for alternative offers sooner or later. In an open market these alternatives are always present. When customers come into contact with such alternatives, turnover that has been traditionally counted on is suddenly swept away. When colleagues act in this way, the infamous short cuts develop in organizations. In this manner organizational responsibilities and authority are stealthily undermined. That is why every supplier (internal or external) must continue to exert himself to safeguard his position. In other words, he should make certain that customers have no reason to seek alternative supplies. This implies that he should innovate to keep his service attractive. Thus this balance measurement reveals *future threats to the present market position*.

Attainability of service vs management and communication

Innovating means constantly looking for ways to improve. This results in the innovation of products and processes. It is, however, a human trait to opt for another route. Sometimes one tries to consolidate a position by bureaucratic means, that is by long and cumbrous procedures with extra links to shackle the client. So it is part of customer orientation to take note of the delays and distortions that the customer encounters when placing his order. These so-called transfer risks can only be prevented by vigilant management. It frequently happens that the customer is not aware of the existence of a particular service within the package, and how he can obtain it. Only clear communication can offer a solution here. A well-performed balance measurement of these issues provides insight into the most important *current threats to the market position*.

USING THE QUALITY SCALES IN PRACTICE: MEASURING QUESTIONS

The preceding has shown that the quality scales are suitable for systematic investigation of existing quality situations. They provide a coherent set of standards for the three pairs of elements described. In this basic form they are an excellent instrument for brainstorming sessions etc. We frequently employ the quality scales in cooperation with management and employees to develop and refine the notion of quality. The scales are tailored for the organization concerned.

A workshop leads to the formulation of verifiable objectives concerning the quality of the service (product specifications) and verifiable objectives concerning quality control (adequate reactions). These can be united in a quality plan. Top management must see to it that there are sufficient cross-connections. For these quality objectives are always formulated at a certain interface, within one customer–supplier relation. The tangible result of this exercise is a coherent quality plan, which also contains the basis for follow-up and verification.

We now descend one more level into the three balance situations. Thus measuring questions emerge for 18 key points, which are interrelated and which suffice to obtain a fairly complete survey of the quality situation at each individual interface. At this detailed level we obtain a useful questionnaire, with which we can quickly carry out an audit.

The key points are shown, once again, on scales. These key points are translated into measuring questions. A short illustration or explanation is given for each question so that its meaning will be clear. If required, the questions can easily be translated to fit a specific situation.

Each question concerning orientation towards the client has a counter-question regarding the reaction of the supplier (question types (a) and

(b) respectively). If the questionnaire is used as an audit instrument, a score can be drawn up by way of a points system. An overall picture is obtained when the scores of the three balance situations on the left side are set off against those on the right side.

Market potential of supplier

This balance situation is shown in figure 5.9.

1 (a) *In what way are clients' needs systematically assessed?*
Possibilities are: complaints registration; registration of response time with regard to complaints; examination of customer satisfaction.

1 (b) *How does the supplier ensure that the choice of the service offered fits the client's wishes?*
Is there a quality planning process that sees to it that the expectations inventoried are actually transformed into accepted objectives for the quality of the product offered? Which responsibilities and competences can be distinguished? How are contributions made visible?

2 (a) *What are the (specific) contents of the client's wishes regarding the primary service to be obtained?*

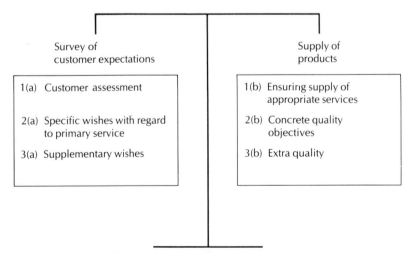

FIGURE 5.9 Determining market potential of supplier

Is a regular inventory of specific wishes part of the quality planning process? Are customers given the opportunity to make their wishes known?

2 (b) *What are the concrete quality objectives for the hard service aspects?* Does the quality planning process lead to a product standard, which defines the quality performance regarding the hard aspects for a 100 per cent score? Has this quality performance been formulated in such a way that it can be verified?

3 (a) *What are the customer's wishes with regard to supplementary services and the way they are marketed?*
Is the client provided with sufficient and clear information about his rights and obligations in connection with the product offered (instructions, warranty, complaints etc.)?

3 (b) *How is the service organized to fit the customer's wishes, including the courtesy aspect?*
Here the issue is to ascertain whether the supplementary product qualities and the extra quality are sufficiently defined and made known to the client. The reasoning here is that a supplier can only distinguish himself positively regarding a vital product, which is also a commodity, by supplying extra quality. For technically a competitor could supply the product at a similar quality level.

Future threats to present market position

This balance situation is shown in figure 5.10.

4 (a) *To what extent are potential competitors and the development of their market influence examined?*
The market position of a supplier is often attractive to others. Potential suppliers will try to disturb this existing balance (often by using short cuts). It is a good thing to anticipate this and chart likely competitors and their market influence. This is a first step to prevent the competitor taking over the market sector.

4 (b) *To what extent does the supplier decide in favour of a particular market sector?*
It is not possible to satisfy all parties concerned to the same extent. The supplier of a service does not have the same interest in every

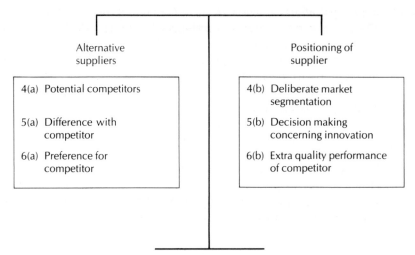

FIGURE 5.10 Determining future threats to present market position

category of potential customers. That is why a conscious choice should be made in favour of a certain market sector, which fits the organizational objectives and the general service strategy. A corresponding service level must be defined for the chosen category (market sector).

5 (a)   *In what way do the services offered by the competition differ from those of the supplier?*
Technically speaking, the services are often not fundamentally different from those offered by the competitor, because of their commodity character. Nevertheless it is a good thing to analyse the differences extensively and to make a principled decision about whether the extras should also be supplied with one's own product. In doing so the notion of excellence can be underlined.

5 (b)   *How is the decision made to adjust the services to the alternative supply which aims at the same market sector?*
Within the chosen market sector and the defined service level one should constantly consider which concrete improvements can be carried out in products and processes. The decision making should be organized separately so that learning, innovative potential is generated inside the organization. In the modern approach innovation can be planned, because one sets up a feasible specification for a certain deadline.

6 (a)   *Which (potential) customers decide in favour of a competitor and why?*
The causes can be many. For instance, the product of the competitor may be technically just a little bit better or easier to use. Here, however, one should also consider the higher performance of the competitor with regard to extra quality. This often determines the customer's choice in a situation where there are no fundamental differences in the service itself.

6 (b)   *How does the supplier find an adequate reaction to the extra performance of the competitor?*
Here the issue is often to consolidate the soft sides of the product. How can one improve the accessibility of the firm, increase the service orientation of the employees? The extra quality performance of the competitor must not become a reason for the customer to defect.

Current threats to market position

This balance situation is shown in figure 5.11.

7 (a)   *To what extent is the (potential) customer familiar with the service package?*
To take an example from the banking sphere: a private account consists of more aspects than merely debit and credit. Informing

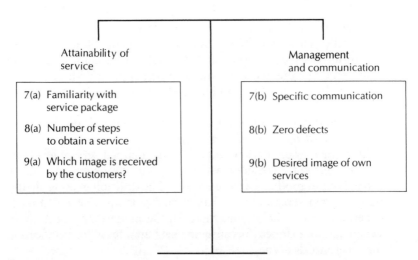

FIGURE 5.11 Determining current threats to market position

the client may lead to his opening a savings account and thus prevent problems in the transfer of payments (e.g. use of a savings account as a pay account).

7 (b) *How does one use publicity to supplement missing knowledge of the service package?*
Is there an advertisement or communication plan which consciously influences the expectations of the client, e.g. by communicating defined messages (the quality standard, the quality promise etc.) to selected target groups?

8 (a) *What steps must a customer take to obtain the service?*
The more steps there are, the greater is the risk of mistakes and irritation. If a customer, after having been put through three times, still isn't connected with the right person to make his wishes known, he will be irritated. The same goes (and even more so) for the number of times he has to pick up his pen or his phone to obtain the promised service.

8 (b) *Is there a systematic check of what goes wrong or what is superfluous in contacts with the customer?*
Do all procedures, methods and equipment fit together perfectly at the same time? Is there systematic detection and analysis of defects? Has the process been organized in such a way that the client can be put through to the correct employee right away?

9 (a) *To what extent does the image the supplier wants to transmit get across to the customer?*
Is it verified whether the desired image of services (e.g. reliability, accessibility, speed of processing an order, high service level) is actually received by the client?

9 (b) *What does the supplier do to transmit the desired image of his services to the customer?*
Is there a consistent publicity policy which ensures that all utterances in the media give a uniform and correct indication of the extent and reliability of the service level?

CONCLUSIONS

Working at excellence in the service industries requires a simple, reliable instrument that can be used throughout the organization. We have discussed an instrument – the quality scales – which charts both external and internal customer orientations and the adequate reaction to these positions.

The central thesis is that a healthy customer–supplier relation is characterized by a balance between the perception of customer wishes and the resulting reactions of the supplier. Each perception (customer orientation) must therefore by definition lead to an (adequate) reaction by the supplier. For each of the quality-determining balance situations, a productive tension is created.

The instrument itself is simple. It involves measuring three balance situations: inventory of customer expectations vs supply of products; alternative suppliers vs positioning of supplier; and noting transfer risks vs management and communication.

The instrument can be used creatively. In its basic form, it can be used to brainstorm in a more general way about the quality control situation. In a very detailed form we use it as an audit to assess a particular service or department. When used for further parts of the organization it promotes unity of ideas. This is a prerequisite for creating the support which is needed to achieve perfection in the entire service organization.

6

Customer orientation within the organization

WILLEM J. VRAKKING

INTRODUCTION: DEFINITION OF INTERNAL CUSTOMER ORIENTATION

In commercial and non-commercial organizations, everyone is supposed to know who their customers are. In most cases they will automatically think of the organization's external customers: those people who purchase and pay for the products or, in the case of services provided by government organizations, the target groups which are to receive or must accept the products.

It must have become clear by now to most organizations that customer orientation is a prerequisite for providing services which are to the clients' satisfaction; this is one of the fundamental rules that Tom Peters has been emphasizing world-wide for the past five years (Peters and Austin, 1985). The realization that we can also distinguish customers within the organization is a recent development. In particular the quality approach in organizations, as espoused in the works of such gurus as Crosby, Juran and Deming, has emphasized the approach of internal customer orientation.

Quality can be defined as *honouring your commitments* regarding your customers' wishes and demands. Your customers are the purchasers of your products and services, and to a large extent they are also located inside your own organization.

The next in line, or the next in the chain, is the next link in the production processes in which you participate. It is no coincidence that

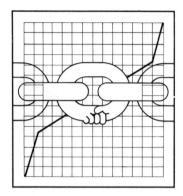

FIGURE 6.1 Philips quality logo

Philips selected the illustration in figure 6.1 to represent its quality programme.

In some organizations (for example KLM) the organization chart places the customers at the top. This reflects the view that the various organizational levels should adopt an attitude which enables others to do their jobs, and ultimately to serve the external customer in the top layer (figure 6.2).

Another company to take this course was SAS, which declared that the external customer ultimately determines the business. In the well-known film about SAS, *50 Million Moments of Truth*, the implications are

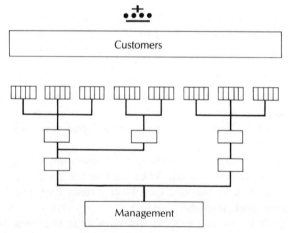

FIGURE 6.2 KLM organization chart

made very clear. Every communication between company and customer, regardless of where it takes place and between whom, must comply with the customer's wishes. For if the customer is not satisfied, he can easily turn to another company; in most cases there are enough options for him to take his business elsewhere. To realize the internal moments of truth, a great deal of internal analysis is necessary and the production processes must be mapped exhaustively.

THE PRIMACY OF THE INTERNAL CUSTOMER

When we start to distinguish our customers internally, as we are already used to doing externally, we will eventually be able to measure our internal quality by the level of their satisfaction. In addition, our creativity will be tested in first trying to determine the exact content of their wishes and subsequently fulfilling them. In this way one of the characteristics of good internal entrepreneurship can thrive.

If the internal customer is placed higher up in the organization, the reaction will often be: 'Of course, I have to do this for that boss.' However, in many cases the next in line will be located not at a higher level of management, but at the same level or at a lower level of staff or operational management. This presents a particular problem in project organizations or matrix organizations, because a customer-oriented attitude is fundamental to the effectiveness of the chosen organizational structure. For only when this customer-oriented attitude is present does an effective internal tuning of the added values of the many participants in a process become possible.

For example, in a multinational enterprise the national sales organizations are often diametrically opposed to the interests of the product-oriented organizations within the same enterprise. The product-oriented subsidiary or division wishes to ensure maximum attention from the national sales organizations for its products. The national sales organizations' primary interest lies in maximizing their turnover and profits, and so they will be inclined to give more attention to those products (possibly from other product divisions) which contribute most to reaching this goal.

The links between these two organizational principles are only recognized by people who are able to monitor both processes, who can balance the diverging interests of their internal customers and serve them. For what should one do when company XYZ's sales organization in Spain has other priorities than the business unit, which is organized along the product axis and which depends on this sales organization for the eventual sales of its products? It was with good reason that Philips recently gave the highest priority to the product divisions, but the question is: does this resolve the dilemma?

Naturally there will be people who say: 'That is all very well, but I have to establish priorities, and I cannot always fulfil the wishes of the next in line – especially if they want something yesterday, while I am working on some other priority. This internal customer may understand my dilemma, but that does not mean he will stop nagging, so I can't satisfy all the internal customers.' And indeed, sometimes people will have to get precedence because of an internal priority, especially when this priority is connected with the most important delivery deadline that the organization must make as a company.

For example, a company in Silicon Valley was started up with venture capital, and had to translate its new computer design into hardware and deliver it to the first buyer within 14 months. To reach this milestone, everybody in the company who worked on the critical path of planning received a red badge which read 'help me'. As soon as one of these red badge bearers approached someone with a question, that person dropped his work in hand and did not rest until he could answer the question or provide the service. In this way the company achieved its goal and revealed both the actual hierarchy in the work and the most important assignment of management, which is to condition and facilitate.

Again, suppose you work in a computer centre and you are asked for help on a project within a certain department of a company division, for which the computer centre was installed in the first place. Choose your reaction from the following:

- 'I haven't got time now, solve your own problems.'

- 'Please apply to my superior in writing.'

- You make an appointment with the person who has the problem to examine what he himself can do towards solving it.

- You organize a different solution internally in your centre.

- You search for a solution outside.

Your customer-oriented mentality will be revealed very rapidly.

INTERNAL CUSTOMER ORIENTATION CAN BE MEASURED

Intra-organizational customer orientation is strongly connected with the degree to which the ever-present internal rivalry between divisions and between people in the organization can be deflected towards a mentality of mutual support in the realization of their work. If your organization scores heavily on the following statements, then readiness to help each other, an attitude of mutual support, will usually be absent to a high degree.

It should not be necessary for the external customer to coordinate us internally

Measuring point: how often does the external customer have to organize us?

One of the most poignant symptoms of the lack of internal customer orientation is when the customer has to put us in touch internally to get his wishes fulfilled (and rightly so). It is not hard to predict the customer's thoughts.

For example, you have to inform your computer supplier's salesman that the service man visited you yesterday and that he came up with some very good ideas for future configurations, which the salesman had not presented. The salesman had good reason not to mention these ideas, but the service department was not aware of this.

The basis should not have to wonder time and time again what the top wants

Measuring point: how often do you organize strategy/tactics meetings for the basis?

Although many boardrooms create the impression of wanting to discuss everything as extensively as possible and to base decisions on those discussions, the consequence will be that neither middle management nor the basis are involved in policy decisions, with corresponding results.

For example, a new automated production system can be introduced by way of the D-day model, in which case resistance is to be expected. An alternative way is the participation method, which will certainly reduce the vicissitudes of introduction (Vrakking, 1988).

The walls are always rebuilt rapidly

Measuring point: what is the frequency of structured consultation? How much do we know about the services of adjacent departments?

One of the largest problems for many organizations is the internal (un)familiarity with the assortment of products and services. Often one knows little about the products and services in other departments, let alone the concept of internal client rating.

As an example, the internal consulting department of one of my clients is in the process of introducing client rating. In this process the consultant asks the customer to complete an evaluation form after the project, containing statements about the consultant such as:

1 He delivers the information requested (a) rapidly enough (b) to a sufficient degree.
2 He makes recommendations which (a) are sufficiently clear (b) are applicable (c) have enough support.
3 He contributes to the implementation (a) energetically enough (b) with sufficient involvement.

DILEMMAS REGARDING CUSTOMER ORIENTATION

In many organizations we observe that people are trained in a way which precludes the development of the internal customer-oriented attitude. The customer-oriented worker is smothered. In these situations, the following dilemmas often have to be resolved.

Product expertise vs market/branch orientation vs issue orientation

Pressure on the internal differentiation of the organization differs considerably, and is caused by completely different considerations concerning which issues have the highest priority for the organization. The employees will have to integrate this, which requires a great effort from them.

General corporate rules vs situational demands

Sometimes actual customer orientation demands an immediate response which goes against the general corporate rules. Should one persist in that case?

Thinking in terms of tasks vs thinking in terms of added value

It is depressing how some people let their job descriptions distract them from what a flexible organization demands. One example is 'That is not my concern, I'll pass on the message', when a real contribution could have been made rapidly.

Monopolistic situation vs competitive setting

Departments that are in a position of being the only ones providing certain services (such as a maintenance division or a computer centre) will often discuss their customers in monopolistic terms. They show little respect for their clients, who have no other option but to turn to them. More and more frequently this situation is resolved by assigning budgetary rights to those internal customers to shop outside the organization, and by simultaneous cutbacks in the internal services department. At the same time, however, there is usually an increase in services, which means a strong net increase in productivity.

PRECONDITIONS FOR INTERNAL CUSTOMER ORIENTATION

Internal customer orientation will not develop spontaneously in any organization; often it will not grow until mutual support has become a strongly pursued value of the company culture.

In the cultural fitness check (an instrument employed by our firm for organizational innovation), this value emerges as a very dominant feature. The cultural score corresponds with the degree to which the organization perceives itself as a high-performing system. If the organization itself does not at least indicate that mutual support is an important issue, realization of internal customer orientation becomes very difficult to sustain.

Research results obtained in The Netherlands show that perception of this support orientation as a *desired* value in the company culture is much higher than perception of the *current* existing level. Figure 6.3 shows the current cultural index scores of several organizations which turned to our bureau for advice. The scores corresponded with their performance: the higher the level of internal support orientation, the higher the organization's performance level.

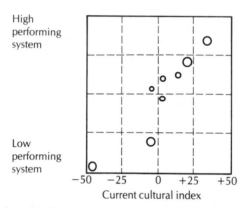

FIGURE 6.3 Cultural index

CONCLUSIONS

We conclude that internal customer orientation can be improved if we are able to change the organization's internal attitude. This attitude depends on whether the organizational culture will adopt *inter alia* a mutual support orientation as a central value.

The degree to which we succeed in building a strong corporate identity within our organization is crucial. In general, it is helpful if the top leads the way. Examples of successful organizations from the service industries possess such an internal culture, which in general is propagated by their top leaders. These leaders must, each in his own way, believe strongly in the necessity of internal customer orientation for the business they are in.

REFERENCES AND FURTHER READING

Cozijnsen, A.J. and Vrakking, W.J. (eds) 1986: *Handboek Strategisch Innoveren* (in Dutch). Kluwer Nive.

van der Hart, H.W.C. 1984: *Supplying without Price Signal* (in Dutch). Nuenen.

Peters, T.J. and Austin, N. 1985: *A Passion for Excellence*. New York: Random House.

Vrakking, W.J. 1985: Revamping organizations through cultural interventions. *Journal of Management Consulting*, 2(3), 10–16.

Vrakking, W.J. 1986: Organizational campaigning (in Dutch). Holland Consulting Group O & I 18.

Vrakking, W.J. (ed.) 1986: *Management of Organizational Innovation* (in Dutch). Vermande.

Vrakking, W.J. 1988: Technological process innovation: impact of the introduction of flexible manufacturing systems on consulting. Presented at the Eighth Annual International Conference of the Strategic Management Society, Winning Strategies for the 1990s, Amsterdam.

7

Marketing of product service: strategic, tactical and operational aspects

HEIN W.C. VAN DER HART

INTRODUCTION

It goes without saying that marketing implies customer orientation. This may be the case in theory, but in practice another picture often emerges: having a marketing department or a marketing manager and using a marketing plan does not automatically mean that the company functions in a customer-oriented fashion. It takes more than that. Hence the marketing of product service is discussed in a broader framework in this contribution. For service organizations in particular, extra attention must be paid to the operational side of marketing, the actual customer orientation in everyday business (van der Hart, 1987).

In marketing literature, product service is an aspect of the marketing mix which has received little attention. In the past few years there have been many publications about the marketing of services, and the subject has also received attention in other ways (Lovelock, 1988). However, the focus of this attention has been on more or less independent types of service, while the services referred to in this chapter primarily form a unit with, or are derived from, the product assortment of an enterprise: pre-sales and after-sales service.

When the term 'service marketing' is used, it generally refers to the marketing of service companies. Obviously, everything which is offered there in terms of specific knowledge and methods is also relevant for the service organization. However, the position of a service department or service organization can deviate strongly from the independent service company. In this contribution we will review the concept of service marketing in a broader context, while taking into account the often extraordinary position of the service organization.

This broad context has to do with the time frame to which we refer when marketing policy is under discussion. In the past, marketeers concentrated mainly on programming the marketing mix, which is a matter of looking ahead over a period of one or two years. More attention is now being paid to strategic marketing, i.e. looking ahead over a period of more than two years with a view to the market. Of course, this is merely looking ahead roughly, and is directed more towards the development of scenarios for market action than to exact predictions of developments. In practice, the latter proves to be a very risky activity.

Recently, under the banner of quality improvement, we have been seeing a sharply increased interest in dealing with customers on the floor, that is during the daily business of the service company. The counter clerk and the client will interact during the process of service; the shopkeeper and his client during the process of orientation and buying; the mechanic and service staff member at the client's during the service process, during the process of complaint intake and during the solving of technical problems. That is where the quality of service is achieved! That is also where the foundation for marketing success is laid. It is exactly this operational side of marketing which has been neglected in marketing literature and theory until now.

For this reason we distinguish three levels in our discussion of service marketing:

- Strategic service marketing
- The service marketing programme
- Operational service marketing.

Successful service marketing is only possible when attention has been paid to all three levels.

STRATEGIC MARKETING OF SERVICE

As mentioned in the introduction, strategic marketing concerns looking ahead over a long period: what will be the marketing position of the company in two or three years' time, and after that? Which long-term marketing strategy is important in this context? The development of a strategic market vision is essential to every organization and also to every service organization or service department.

This prevents the organization being surprised by developments in dynamic markets, developments at competitors and developments in technology at too late a stage. Strategic marketing is focused on having scenarios prepared for all the market situations which might occur in the foreseeable future.

Among the most important questions in strategic marketing are:

- Which position should our organization take in the market?
- Which basic marketing strategy will be relevant?
- Which market trends are relevant?
- What are the competitors' strategies?
- What will be our company's position on the market in three years' time?
- What will be our competitive advantage, our distinctive capacity in relation to our competitors in the years ahead?
- Which opportunities does the market offer and which of our company's strengths are in line?
- Which threats occur and which weaknesses deserve to be reinforced or compensated?

This is only a selection of questions which need to be answered in the context of strategic marketing. The answers will be based on market research data, competitor analysis and internal information systems.

Service positioning from the customer's perspective

For the service organization, the strategic question 'What is our service organization's position?' soon emerges, preceded by the question 'How does the customer view the service offered?' In this context, the following perceptions by the customers are conceivable:

1 Service is barely noticeable to the customer: it is an integral part of the product and it remains within the company.
2 Service is noticeable to the client but is not a primary part of the product offer.
3 Service is noticeable to the client and is just as important as the product itself.

4 Service is more important to the client than the product offered: the product is no longer of primary importance, but is a derived part of the offer.
5 There is no longer a tangible product; only service remains.

Strategic marketing implies constantly asking ourselves which exact position our service will put us in.

For example, buyers of commercial vehicles see service as an essential part of the product offer. It partly determines their choice of supplier. A transport company's primary concern is deploying a truck to the fullest and keeping it on the road.

In time, companies can be transformed from typical product suppliers into service suppliers. At first, service is a cost item; then it evolves into a marketing instrument; and finally it develops into an independent profitable business. This transformation demands an enormous change, and these developments should be detected in time. It is the market that determines the position of the service organization. The market demands more service. The market demands service made to measure, i.e. more specialized service. The company may react to this demand on time; it may be able to anticipate this manifesting need; it may even create that need (Canton, 1988).

An example is a supplier of agricultural equipment who has shifted from selling machines to hiring out agricultural equipment. Another example is the computer market, where hardware has slowly but surely become subordinate to the supply of software and programming services; the product is reduced in importance to a part of a combined package of products and services. Again, leasing results in the concrete product being replaced by a service process, in which commitments regarding available transport capacity have become the main object of the exchange transaction; only service remains. Recently a considerable number of manufacturers have become highly successful in the service sector.

On the other hand, there are also products and markets where service is of little interest to the customer. Service may be touched upon briefly during the actual purchase, for example when buying furniture and clothing. In certain cases service has been reduced to zero, as with disposables and throwaways such as cheap watches and the linen in hospitals (Canton, 1988; Lele, 1986).

Service positioning from the organization's perspective

On the basis of recognition of trends with regard to these five alternatives, a strategic answer will have to be developed. This can drastically change an organization. Some relevant options are:

1 Service as an internally oriented and supportive unit, for example the internal maintenance service.
2 Service as a profit centre within the company, for example the business unit 'service and parts'.
3 Service as an independent or privatized unit with a separate image to the market and a strategy of its own, for example the General Purchasing Bureau of the Dutch government which has been transformed into a private company.
4 Contracting out of service to third parties, for example independent catering companies.

The customer's service perception and the service organizational model can be set out as in figure 7.1, which outlines the strategic options more clearly.

The purpose of this diagram is to show the connection between market and organization. Some explanation will clarify this. When the service is not or barely visible to the customer (100 per cent product), the service department will have a hard time becoming more independent. In that case they will first have to realize a clear profile on the market. However, contracting out to third parties is a low-risk option for the producer. The internal service unit will have to keep recognizing this risk and should act accordingly; it is a threat that must be considered a real one at all times.

As soon as service becomes a visible part of the offer to the customer in the market, a different situation develops for the product supplier. Service will more clearly influence not only profitability but also market share. The own service group more or less determines competitive strength. Service is no longer a cost item but a marketing instrument, and it can even develop into a (profitable) 'business' via a phase in which it is regarded as a separate profit centre. Service can even push the original product into the background completely. Then the reverse situation occurs: service can become independent more and more easily, and it is even possible that a decision is made to contract out the original production.

Summing up, it can be said that the organizational positioning of the

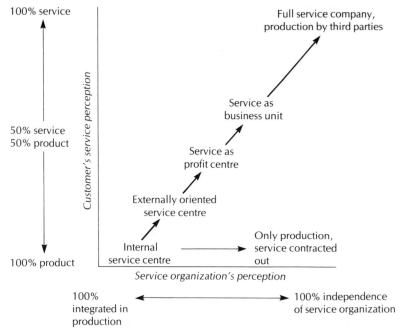

FIGURE 7.1 Strategic options from the product supplier's perspective

service unit cannot be viewed separately from the image that the client has of service. This image is a precondition for the choice between strategic options.

For years, a medium construction company submitted proposals to potential principals about installations which were custom designed for the clients. These proposals demanded a lot of analysis, design and calculation; they could be regarded as pre-sales service. The return was low: only 10 per cent of the quotations resulted in orders. It was also observed that a lot of lost orders were subsequently executed by small construction firms who used the know-how laid down in the proposal. After considering the cost of the lost orders, the company decided to charge a fee for this service, and offered to reimburse potential clients for the fee if an order was placed. In this way the service was visible to the potential customer as a separate element. This measure resulted in an increased return on the proposals that led to orders. However, there was an unexpected additional outcome: it turned out that there was a market for this service, as a result of which a separate business could be developed. In time this became an independent engineering agency alongside the construction company. The turnover and profitability of the engineering agency increased strongly; in the end it became the most important business of the company (van Ruiten and van der Hart, 1983).

These strategic choices need to be weighed against the background of trends and developments in the service market. The distinctive advantage in relation to competitors can also be a motive to decide in favour of a shift on the grid in a well-considered direction.

Total clarity about the marketing aspects mentioned earlier is absolutely imperative, because it matters greatly to the marketing programme (see below) whether service forms an integral part of the product supplier's market offer or is a completely separate activity. This could for example have drastic consequences for the price of service.

SERVICE MARKETING PROGRAMME

Determination of the marketing programme is in fact the traditional essence of service marketing. The key is the marketing mix which, for the service organization, consists of product, price, promotion, location and personnel. The programme is described in a marketing plan.

Service or service product

The service product consists of a number of dimensions or characteristics which are used to give the service its shape and which provide the supplier with the freedom to adjust his offer to meet market developments. The following product dimensions can be distinguished in product service (Nederlandse Vereniging voor Service Management, 1985).

Time

Time obviously plays an important role in the service process. It offers every opportunity to distinguish oneself from competitors, in repair time, travel time from client to service centre, response time, waiting times and handling times.

For an industrial customer who uses a computer, the major part of his costs is the work time lost as a consequence of the breakdown of the equipment. Lele (1986) calls this part of the costs variable costs, as opposed to the fixed costs of service such as actual repair costs. These variable costs depend on the supplier's performance in terms of time.

Safeguards

These safeguards refer to the life cycle of the product, the supply of parts, the availability of equipment, replacement equipment in case of breakdowns etc., guarantees, prevention and availability of service.

For example, a haulage company will depend on the delivery of parts for its trucks during a life cycle of 10 to 15 years. The commercial vehicle producer will have to guarantee this.

Information

One important element which keeps emerging in all types of service is information. The quality of service is determined to a large degree by the information which is given to the customer prior to, during and after the service process. We can compare it, for example, to the patient in hospital whose convalescence can be substantially stimulated when he or she receives information in an adequate way about his or her condition. Hospitals frequently fail in this respect. Sometimes the information is presented in such a way that the patient is unable to grasp its significance. It is no different for product service. Separate information can be provided for:

- Time

- Price

- Repairs

- Operation of the equipment

- Further service options

Much of the irritation of customers about service concerns their dissatisfaction with what is said and promised about products and relevant service. Incorrect information creates incorrect expectations.

Continuity

Continuity concerns the supplier's guarantee to the customer that he will continue to be able to provide service for a specified period.

Know-how

The service organization acquires and secures know-how. Of course, this know-how has everything to do with the quality of service personnel.

Service products can be described well in terms of these five elements, and concrete form is given to one's options for achieving a distinct advantage over competitors. The five dimensions reflect the general product offer. However, it is self-evident that it is possible to differentiate the product offer further according to the nature of the service provided:

Prior to purchase Advice, documentation, training, financing.

During and immediately after the purchase Installation, training, operation instructions, treatment of complaints.

After the purchase Delivery of parts, restoring breakdowns, maintenance and repairs.

Price

Price is the classical marketing instrument, and in the case of service it also has a role in the total marketing mix. Service price policy always entails an imputation problem because in general hourly rates are used. It also depends on costs, although the commercial price should not be determined by costs alone. The customer's perception of the fairness of the price, and how it compares with competing prices, plays an important part. Usually it is not a matter of 'Is the product too expensive?'; in most cases the key question is how the price relates to the quality of the product offered. Service can be expensive, but only on condition that quality is provided – and there must be a demand, backed up by purchasing power, for that extra quality.

Promotion

The marketing instrument of promotion comprises all actions which aim at enhancing the reputation of the service organization and the image or position of the service organization on the market. For example:

- Brochures
- Direct mailing

- Advertisements
- Participation and presentation at exhibitions and fairs
- Internal company communication
- Slide series about the organization and service process
- Articles in professional journals by service experts
- Publicity in the media
- Presentations
- Receptions and guided tours at the company's premises for clients and other reference groups
- Sponsoring.

Public relations is interwoven with these promotion instruments, and more or less constitutes a marketing instrument within the field of promotion.

Location

It is important to identify all locations, occasions and intermediaries outside the service organization where customers have the opportunity of getting in contact with the service organization, such as:

- Dealer network
- Agent network
- Consultants and other experts who can influence the customer's opinion
- Toll-free phone numbers for complaints and information
- Cooperating and related suppliers and their subsidiaries
- Referring authorities and information institutions
- Buyers or service centres of large clients, who maintain a firm relationship with the service organization.

The public image of the service organization is partly determined by all these points of contact.

Personnel

In service marketing it is common to consider personnel to be a separate part of the marketing mix. For the quality of the service provided by service companies is determined to a very large extent by its personnel. Personnel is a marketing instrument that can be influenced by the direction and strategy of recruitment and selection, as well as by the introduction of personnel to the company and the training and career guidance within the company.

One important element of the service product is the interaction between the customer and the supplier of services. It is during this interaction that the quality of the service is determined and the basis for repeat purchasing of services can be laid. We will return to this in the section on operational service marketing.

The marketing plan

The service marketing programme is laid down in a marketing plan which is drawn up step by step. To develop and realize a marketing plan, a service organization will have to take a number of steps. These steps are aimed at achieving continuity in the service organization's performance in the context of its interaction with the market. The marketing cycle we have in mind is shown in figure 7.2.

Marketing at the programme level implies continuous improvement in dealing with the dynamics which also characterize service markets. The main function of the marketing plan is to communicate the marketing strategy in a clear and convincing manner to each and every employee in the organization. In service organizations in particular, it is very important that everyone knows which position is chosen by the organization on the market: what does the service organization stand for? Figure 7.2 also shows which characteristics and skills are of importance for each step in the marketing planning cycle: analytical ability, creativity and communicative skills. In each phase the emphasis differs.

The final step in the marketing planning cycle comprises marketing control: the critical monitoring of service performance by means of control instruments and methods, such as customer questionnaires and customer evaluations. Analysis of complaints and other forms of performance and quality measurement are the points of access for adaptations to the marketing mix. Quality control in service organizations always starts with the customer. His statements about service determine the level of our quality.

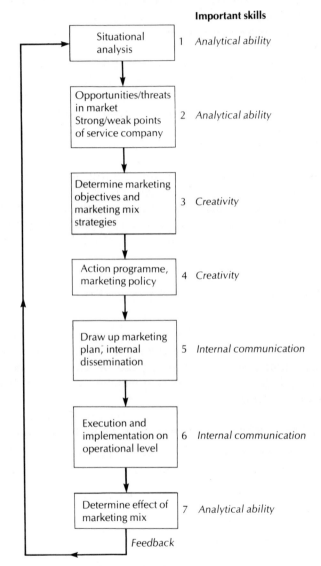

Important skills

Situational analysis	1	*Analytical ability*
Opportunities/threats in market Strong/weak points of service company	2	*Analytical ability*
Determine marketing objectives and marketing mix strategies	3	*Creativity*
Action programme, marketing policy	4	*Creativity*
Draw up marketing plan, internal dissemination	5	*Internal communication*
Execution and implementation on operational level	6	*Internal communication*
Determine effect of marketing mix	7	*Analytical ability*

Feedback

FIGURE 7.2 Planning cycle programme level

For example, a chain-store company enlists the services of so-called mystery shoppers. These are anonymous customers who observe critically how service takes place and who report their experiences to the market research office, which in turn gives feedback on the total picture obtained to the marketing department of the chain-store company (van Minden, 1988).

Volvo Car regularly and intentionally goes out looking for Volvo drivers who have complaints, because there is always a lot to be learned from such people. Most customers who have complaints prefer not to be moaners, so actively seeking out complaints yields a lot more information than passively waiting for them to come in. Furthermore, by this method product defects or weak links in the chain of service can be detected much sooner.

What is also important in marketing control, of course, is that the complaint picture and customer impressions are fed back to the people who provide service at the base of the organization, so that they can adjust their service behaviour in the direction desired by the customer. With that we have come to the third level of marketing of service.

OPERATIONAL SERVICE MARKETING

As was stated at the beginning of this chapter, operational service marketing comprises the daily activities in the interaction with customers. Operational service marketing can be said to be more or less equal to what is meant by customer orientation in service. It refers to the following activities:

- The manner in which service personnel communicate with customers

- The way in which the service organization in general deals with customers: providing information, service planning and so on

- Handling and registration of complaints by the service organization

- Monitoring service customers and equipment to be serviced

- Telephone communication with customers

- Written communication with customers

- Monitoring of the customer relationship by the canvassers and salesmen of services.

Operational service marketing has everything to do with quality of service. When we make the concept of quality operational, we come to the proposition that the quality of service is determined mainly by the customers' perception of that service. That is why, in principle, each quality action in service starts with the customers, and with service personnel carefully observing customers' conduct and customers' responses.

Consulting customers about the assessment of separate elements of service, for instance by way of a questionnaire, usually yields a lot of information, which can be used to start a quality action. The image of the service organization is determined to a large extent by the personal contacts between customers and organization, and after that by the contact between (ex-)customers and potential customers and between customers themselves. We obviously do not control this process completely. That is why control and monitoring of the interaction between customer and service provider is an essential operational aspect of service marketing.

How can we control and monitor this operational process? Several issues are of importance:

1 Adequate *recruitment and selection* of service personnel is essential. It should be very clear to the candidates beforehand which rules of conduct the organization uses in contacts with customers. Recruiting service personnel who do not fit into this formula, which is used with regard to customer orientation in the service organization, irrevocably implies a threat to the future position on the service market: competitors may recruit the right people and will therefore distinguish themselves in a positive way compared with our service organization.

2 A lot of attention to the *introduction* for new service personnel is a must. As well as a general introduction, there must also be thorough training in dealing with customers. We should not let new people find their own way in this field, and in practice the lack of time and necessary personal attention often prevents on-the-job training.

3 *Training* existing personnel in customer-oriented working methods in service is essential. In training courses, such methods must be demonstrated and practised by means of practical examples from daily business and audiovisual aids. For the implementation of quality concepts, methods have been developed which have been applied not only in industry but also in government services (Ezerman, 1986).

4 *Internal communication* is also an important instrument to feed back experiences with customers and to achieve a customer-oriented formula of your own. Poor internal communication leads to a lack

of opportunities for service personnel to correct and readjust their own working methods. There is a need for exchanging experiences, but there is no opportunity. Experiences with and complaints from customers should be open to discussion within the service organization. That is why explicit attention to internal communication is very important in the context of operational service marketing.

5 Formulating a *work model and rules of conduct* for the role of the person who provides service can provide both clarity and motivation to work using a well-thought-out customer-oriented formula.

For example, a computer centre within a large organization developed an instrument for measuring, on a regular basis, users' opinions concerning 28 elements of service. A classification of attention points was derived from this, based on the users' scores for each separate element of service. In that way insight was gained into the strong and weak points of the service provided. The results of the quality measurement were fed back to the service personnel. During these evaluation meetings, measures and pointers were developed for the purpose of improving the quality of service and obtaining a better score from the customers with regard to quality.

A second example concerns the maintenance department of a large enterprise with many subsidiaries all over The Netherlands. A two-day conference on the quality of the technical projects department was organized, where management and departmental heads gave concrete form to the concept of quality based on insights into service marketing. Subsequently, in several meetings, all employees of the department were confronted with a simple work model and ten concrete rules of conduct, which were illustrated by means of cartoons on wall panels. On the basis of these ten items the bottlenecks in the service process were discussed. This resulted in the forming of work groups that studied a number of recorded and selected main bottlenecks in order to develop solutions. This entire programme, based on the principles of service marketing, led to a reinforcement of the customer orientation of both the organization and the department personnel. Moreover management, who were present at all meetings, found the communication with employees in these quality meetings very illuminating, and the experience provided them with new insights and impressions. Service marketing was the key to providing a concrete framework for the quality of service.

Service marketing and quality of service are the complementary elements of what we call operational marketing: maintaining customer orientation in the interaction between customer and service personnel, in order to distinguish the service organization from competitors in this market.

REFERENCES

Canton, I.D. 1988: How manufacturers can move into the service business. *Journal of Business Strategy*, July/August, 40–4.

Ezerman, G.C. 1986: *Quality Improvement in Government Service* (in Dutch). The Hague: VUGA.

Lele, M.M. 1986: How service needs influence product strategy. *Sloan Management Review*, no. 3.

Lovelock, Chr. H. 1988: *Managing Services: marketing operations and human resources.* Englewood Cliffs: Prentice-Hall.

Nederlandse Vereniging voor Service Management, 1985: *Service Department as Profit Centre* (in Dutch). Bussum.

van der Hart, H.W.C. 1987: Marketing: bridging the distance between theory and practice (in Dutch). *Holland Harvard Review*, no. 12, autumn, 111–18.

van Minden, J. 1988: Mystery shoppers research (I) and (II). *Tijdschrift voor Marketing*, nos 9 and 10.

van Ruiten, J.H.S. and van der Hart, H.W.C. 1983: Smooth industrial marketing. *Tijdschrift voor Marketing*, no. 17, 26–31.

8

Visible results for invisible services

WILLEM F.G. MASTENBROEK

INTRODUCTION

Today's degree of competition in business compels a company to aim at performance, cost awareness, quality and customer orientation. Political pressures and scarce resources are pushing government and non-profit organizations in this direction as well.

When linked to certain organizational conditions, a management information system in the form of indicators that regularly make visible the results of organizational units can greatly contribute to this. Utilizing such a system will mean feeding results back to units in the organization.

This chapter presents examples of indicators that are used as management information in five business areas. I will focus on the service sector; this includes service elements of production activities, and corporate departments providing services to internal clients. The reasons for focusing on services are first the growing importance of this sector, and secondly the difficulty in developing indicators for service elements. The objective measurement of output is not always possible, and more subjective measures won't work unless they have been accepted.

I will also describe the criteria that such information should meet and the pitfalls that may occur in its use. Finally, I will discuss the organizational conditions in which this type of information can thrive.

PERFORMANCE INDICATORS FOR MANAGEMENT INFORMATION

Administrative automation tends to produce an over-abundance of information and indicators. The main problem in information management is selection: how to condense the available information into a few figures that offer a true informational handle to management and employees. Ideally, each unit and each level of the organization should have a limited number of available indicators that will periodically make visible the results obtained. Measuring results in this way provides a constant incentive for improving performance, because it mobilizes energy: units know what they stand for.

Many organizations have a long history of using indicators of all kinds, and it would seem simple enough to achieve this ideal. But actual practice has shown such an achievement to be far from simple. Here are a few examples of performance indicators.

Retail trade

- Queuing at cash desks
- Complaints
- Turnover per department or article group and per square metre
- Sales costs per square metre.

A central marketing department

- The contribution of new products to the operating result: volume times margin
- Evaluation of the service to the sales departments by sales managers, rating factors such as level of expertise, speed and communication on a scale from excellent to poor, and adding subjective comments.

A production department

- Percentage of deliveries outside specifications
- Percentage exceeding delivery time
- Absenteeism.

A distribution centre

- Delivery time
- Delivery reliability
- Complaints.

Business services

Per project, the client scores the following on a four-point scale:

- Quality of information asked
- Quality of solutions
- Commitment and involvement of the service supplier.

In all sectors, assessment forms for clients (whether internal or external) are sometimes used as an aid in information collection. The periodic measurements are frequently shown by graphs, which promote a lucid presentation and make the overall trend visible at a glance.

These examples are deceptively simple. Managers must generally hold discussions, taking several meetings, before they arrive at a limited number of indicators. Sometimes the clients, the consumers of the products or services, may play a role in the decision-making process. Interestingly enough, in several cases qualitative measurements are used to obtain periodic insight into the assessment of internal or external clients; this is not surprising when one considers the increasing importance of such matters as quality and client orientation. Time and time again, the commitment of top management – and at times the pressure of competing organizations – is ultimately required before this development is initiated.

CRITERIA FOR INDICATORS

Employees and managers must perceive the indicators as their own instruments. Too often people have the feeling that these instruments are prescribed by top management and will ultimately be used as a means of control; the result is a paper system that is not taken particularly seriously and rapidly loses its credibility. This implies that the employees involved must have a say in the choice and the use of the indicators. This process is supported if examples are provided and if all kinds of records and standards are already available in the organization. In the final analysis, the choice of the most crucial yardsticks is their own. Of course, the performance indicators that are chosen must fit in with company strategies and goals.

Operationalizing the measures chosen, keeping them up to date, and periodically supplying the information do not come naturally. Some of the examples are straightforward enough, while others (for instance, the logistic performance indicators) will require a great deal of effort before one arrives at usable operationalizations. Even a matter such as recording complaints seems quite simple, but it is only effective with a good code system that at least indicates what area bears responsibility for a complaint.

Thus we already have a few important criteria for indicators. They should be:

Acceptable Indicators must be accepted by those involved. This means that although the framework is handed down from above, it is very important that the individuals who will use the indicators have a say in their ultimate choice, design and use.

Simple and visible Indicators must provide easily reproducible information. It is helpful if you can start from information that has already been recorded; if it is a big job to get the information together, it won't work. 'Simple' also means limited in number; a long list of indicators is a sign of weakness, and the number should be restricted to three or four. 'Visible' chiefly means tangible, in the sense of showing trends that are capable of being represented graphically.

Capable of being influenced and motivational Only if people feel that they themselves can influence the results of the measurements will the indicators be meaningful and motivating. This means that indicators must lie largely within particular fields of responsibility.

These dos and don'ts are not exhaustive. Table 8.1 provides a concise summary of the don'ts and dos of working with indicators.

ORGANIZATIONAL DESIGN

Performance indicators are only of value if units bear clear responsibility for specific result areas. Extensive functional differentiation is an obstacle

TABLE 8.1 The don'ts and dos of working with indicators

Don'ts

Bureaucratization
Cynicism
Scores are used for control
Perfectionism
Impatience
Internal professionalism
Relationship of indicators to organizational culture is underestimated
Management's attention slackens

Dos

Ingrain them in the line organization
Use scores as a platform to improve results
Absolute figures are unimportant; the trend is what counts
Learn from mistakes: do not blame another, but ask
　'What can I do about it?'
Use proven techniques of problem solving and decision making
Develop good vertical communication and involvement of higher echelons
Develop the quality of horizontal cooperation

---

in this respect; it dissipates responsibility and makes it fairly easy to pass complaints to other links in the production chain.

There is a trend towards basing differentiation within organizations less on functional specializations and more on product/market combinations. The resulting units have a comparatively high level of functional integration; nonetheless, most organizations will still have some units that do not supply end products as output to external clients. In this context, the organization will use the principle of an internal client orientation. The next in line becomes the market and must be viewed as a client. Some of the indicators described above show this. It may also mean that price tickets are put on internal supplies.

Another solution is to free units of the obligation to use services and products from their own firm. If a unit feels that it can obtain the same service or product cheaper and better elsewhere, it is free to do so. This draws the market mechanism into the organization all the way to the central departments.

One mechanism that is sometimes introduced is 'learning from another'. In my view, this is one of the most promising ways of gaining from the information collected. Learning takes place at different levels:

first, units hold internal consultation about the results obtained, particularly about the methods of improving them; and secondly, similar units in the organization (for example, branches of the same company) compare results. This process is then combined with the exchange of ideas and experiences. Such interaction calls for excellent interpersonal relations; the quality of communication often becomes one of the major elements of a project to improve services and to raise customer satisfaction. Measuring performance is the driving force, but an ever-increasing emphasis is put on people relations and team development, and on the skills of problem solving, decision making and constructive negotiating. A schematic rendering of the mechanism is shown in figure 8.1: with the passage of time, results become increasingly dependent on the quality of communication.

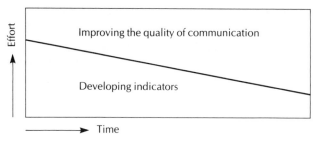

FIGURE 8.1 The importance of communication

The organizational design that comes into focus can best be described as follows. An organization is composed of relatively autonomous units with products and clients of their own. The units' results are regularly made visible, and the units are provided with feedback. Relations among the units themselves stimulate both the mutual exchange of results and joint efforts to improve those results. Clarity about common goals and high-quality vertical and horizontal communication contribute to this.

This organizational design is linked to a theoretical concept, that of organizations as networks of units balancing autonomy and interdependency. Particular patterns of autonomy and interdependency show a strong competitive power. A general characteristic of these patterns is the articulation of autonomy as well as interdependency in the relationship among units. Examples of incentives are shown in table 8.2. The organizational form is both central and decentral. The incentives promote a certain balance between units; this balance raises positive dynamics and sustains a commitment to improve results. This concept is described in chapter 2. Elsewhere (Mastenbroek 1987, 1988) the interventions and programmes that are needed to develop this type of organization have been elaborated.

TABLE 8.2 Balance of tension between autonomy and interdependency: examples of incentives

Autonomy	Interdependency
Profit centres with a large degree of independence in internal structure, investments, product development and market strategy	Company facilities and guidelines in fields such as research, risk capital, management development and financial systems
Flatter hierarchy	Horizontal mobility
Encouraging initiatives and experiments	Safety net for risk takers
Team spirit, management by walking around	Clear mission, we-feeling, house style, informal atmosphere
Continual feedback and comparison of results per unit	Increasing mutual effectiveness by learning from one another
Us versus the internal competitor	Us versus the external competitor

REFERENCES

Mastenbroek, W.F.G. 1987: *Conflict Management and Organization Development*. Chichester, New York: Wiley.

Mastenbroek, W.F.G. 1988: A dynamic concept of revitalization. *Organizational Dynamics*, spring, 52–61.

PART III

Experiences and problem areas

9

Quality and customer orientation in a technical department: a case study of service marketing

HEIN W.C. VAN DER HART

INTRODUCTION

This case study describes the process of organizational change as it took place in the Department of Technical Projects (DTP) of Royal Ahold Inc. Royal Ahold is the largest food retailer in The Netherlands. The DTP is an internal technical service and maintenance organization.

The study starts at the end of 1984, when the department had just undergone a reorganization which created considerable internal unrest. We describe the consecutive steps which were taken to develop the department from an operational body into a service group, which implies a fundamentally different way of functioning.

The case description starts with an analysis of the situation. We then describe how, from a marketing approach, working in a customer-oriented manner was introduced to management team and middle management. Subsequently we address the next step, where the customer is the central issue, in which all employees are involved in the change process. We then describe the follow-up, and also the way in which continuity in the safeguarding of customer orientation is realized. The next logical step is the process in which the notion of customer orientation is applied to internal relationships; with this we conclude the case study.

SITUATIONAL ANALYSIS

The Department of Technical Projects was established in 1974. Before that date the DTP worked exclusively in Ahold's retail subsidiaries; from 1974 the group had to start providing maintenance and technical services to all Ahold company units in The Netherlands. The DTP offered a wide variety of mostly constructional and maintenance services, ranging from project management for new construction, renovations and alterations to preventive maintenance and the remedy of technical malfunctions.

The DTP consisted of approximately 120 employees, mostly from a technical or an engineering background. The department exhibited the typical characteristics of this type of organization: it was a relatively introverted group whose main focus was on the purely technical aspects of the work. It was a classical product-oriented internal department, and had the following image within the organization:

- No customer orientation

- On-time delivery

- Special wishes difficult to realize

- Technical requirements too high

- Too expensive

- Undesirable monopoly position within the Ahold organization.

In 1979 a new manager was put in charge of the DTP. The early 1980s saw a reorganization of the department – the so-called 'Repositioning 1982–1984'. The major issues were:

- The department had to become *self-supporting*.

- The department had to become *customer oriented* by means of appointing account groups for the major Ahold companies.

- The department had to operate more *professionally* by means of account management, project management, definition of tasks and training.

- The department had to be able to compete with and be constantly *tested* against external suppliers of technical and maintenance services.

Technically and functionally the reorganization was completed in 1984, but what was still lacking is best described as the right working climate and organizational culture. Furthermore, several questions remained concerning the actual filling-in of functions.

The management team, which had been installed and functioned as such, contemplated the situation and decided to introduce a programme aimed at the quality of service and marketing of technical and maintenance services, to provide the missing piece. Through the concerted action of the management team, the head of the department of training and organization, the responsible personnel officer and an external senior management consultant, a first step was developed: a two-day seminar titled 'Marketing of service DTP Ahold'.

MARKETING OF SERVICES AS POINT OF DEPARTURE FOR ORGANIZATIONAL CHANGE

In developing the seminar, several principles and objectives were involved:

1 Knowledge and understanding of the principles of service marketing were to be obtained.
2 The seminar had to contribute to practical application and to its dissemination throughout the organization.
3 The seminar had to contain reflections from client situations.
4 The management team and the entire middle management were invited to the seminar. Attendance by all the people in this group had to be ensured, and it was especially important to make sure that nobody in the organization felt passed over.
5 A certain amount of fatigue regarding organizational change had to be taken into account. The seminar had to find the right balance between the feelings of 'something new again' on the one hand, and 'we've heard this all before' on the other.

In view of these basic assumptions, the seminar contained the following elements:

1 A carefully prepared introduction by the head of the DTP, as well as discussion of the programme by the head of the department of training and organization.
2 An introduction on the principles of service marketing, including exercises and discussion.

3 'The customer has the floor.' In a relaxed atmosphere, an important customer (from one of the Ahold companies) talked about his experiences with a constructional project executed by the DTP. This was followed by a lively discussion with the customer.
4 Further discussions concerning this dialogue.
5 For the purpose of achieving a follow-up, three groups addressed the following themes:
   (a) Information about customers and evaluation of the work
   (b) Communication with the client
   (c) Marketing strategy, planning and internal communication.

The head of the DTP did not take part in the discussions; he acted as an observer. He made comments on the reports by the subgroups, and he provided a summary which included the external consultant's reaction.

The seminar had the desired effect on the participants, on the understanding that the aim was to carefully prepare a correct follow-up in the DTP organization. The seminar concluded with the setting up of three working groups:

• 'Follow-up in the DTP organization', which was responsible for a follow-up programme

• 'Score where it is already possible', aimed at fast and very visible changes which would keep the feeling of result alive

• 'Communication', which was concerned with both external and internal communication.

A follow-up conference was scheduled for the beginning of 1985.

The aspect of communication gives cause for a marginal note. Defective internal communication has been talked about often before, but returns time and time again. It is important that internal communication is considered again, but this time in the new context of the principle of customer orientation. External communication with customers is only possible if internal communication is sound. Thinking from the customer's perspective will bring the employees into one line for adequate internal communication; the customer is the common denominator for internal communication.

DISSEMINATION OF CUSTOMER ORIENTATION THROUGHOUT THE ORGANIZATION

The follow-up of the two-day seminar was taken up energetically, which proved the positive effect of the seminar. Every seminar participant contributed actively to the follow-up: nobody disappeared behind the scenes, nobody was allowed to pull out. Two days were programmed for the further dissemination of customer orientation, which all employees without exception were obliged to attend. Groups of 20 to 25 employees were formed.

The first day was aimed at introducing the marketing philosophy in a practical form, and at exchanging experiences with customers and discussing bottlenecks in the organization. The second day, which took place one month later, was intended to translate the information presented during the first day into practice, and also to offer solutions to the bottlenecks.

During the first day, the manager of the DTP presented an introduction for all the groups, to clarify the objectives of the programme. He was present at all meetings. This constituted a unique opportunity for both him and the employees to exchange ideas extensively. The management team and middle management performed as trainers, to which end a short introduction 'Train the trainer' was provided prior to the two days. The entire training programme went under the name of 'Quality of service', because technicians have more affinity for the concept of quality than the notion of marketing.

The composition of the groups was a subject of discussion. The decision was made to form groups of a mixed composition for the first day, in which functions and echelons were completely mixed together. On the second day, which was aimed at individuals' working fields, there were functional groups: bringing together in one group as many participants as possible who have to work together on a daily basis.

As was mentioned before, all employees – none excepted – were invited to the group meetings; this included telephone operators and administrative employees. For all of them deal with clients.

Several aids were developed for the first day. All participants received a concise explanation of the concepts of quality of service, the marketing of the DTP and customer-oriented functioning. This was elaborated in ten points for customer orientation and a model, which together provided a manual on dealing with customers. Cartoons on large panels illustrated the ten points visually. These panels were posted in the room where the course was held. In addition the participants received a small practical card containing both the ten quality points (summarized) and the work model (see figure 9.1). The external consultant provided the outline and formulated both the ten quality points and the work model. The DTP (naturally) prepared the visualization and the quality card.

Quality points

1 Customer is central.
2 No uninvited amateurism.
3 Stay in the customer's picture.
4 Customer-friendly organizing.
5 Who is the customer?
6 We are all involved in DTP marketing.
7 Thinking along with the customer in Ahold context.
8 Be clear to the customer.
9 At the customer's, do only customer business.
10 Listen and be receptive to customer signals.

Work model

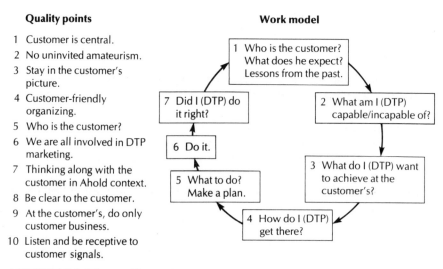

FIGURE 9.1 The quality card

For the second day of the course, ten main issues and bottlenecks were distilled from the reactions which were gathered on the first day. Furthermore, a case description was prepared which was used as exercise material during the second day. On this second day, subgroups worked at finding solutions for one or several bottlenecks. Each subgroup chose one or several main bottlenecks from the list of ten issues. The ten issues were as follows:

1 Who is the customer? Who determines our work?
2 What attitude do we adopt in regard to customer wishes? How do we decide what we will and what we won't do?
3 The customer is the victim of our defective internal communication and cooperation.
4 Improve the ways of examining the effect of our work on the client (evaluation).
5 Promotion towards the customer is underdeveloped.
6 Our workload leaves us no time for marketing.
7 Preparation, completion and transfer of projects to the customer is not effective.

8 Handling complaints.
9 The customer does not see the advantages of preventive maintenance.
10 Observing rules, standards and procedures for the benefit of the
customer.

The second day began with feedback of the results of the first day, and
the announcement of improvement issues which were to be realized
soon. Because expectations were clearly raised on the first day, it was of
major importance that results were shown as soon as possible. This
meant that the programme would be taken more seriously.

The experiences with both quality/marketing days were remarkable:

1 On the first day, management learnt a great deal about what went
on down in the organization in the relation between DTP and
customers.
2 Because the focus was on the customer, there was much more
emphasis on relations with the customer than on functioning in
relation to colleagues. The former was a less sensitive area.
3 The first day yielded an enormous reaction; no fewer than 73
bottlenecks, attention points and remarks were taken down.
4 Expectations for the future were raised.
5 Everybody was aware of being involved and of having a say in
determining the image of the DTP.
6 On the second day the participants actually worked on solutions
which could be used immediately; this resulted in their feeling even
more productive than on the first day.
7 The theme of internal communication and mutual cooperation in
relation to the customer was chosen to work on more often than
other themes.

CONTINUITY IN QUALITY AND MARKETING

By the middle of 1985 the programme 'Quality of service and marketing'
was completed. A large number of concrete suggestions for improvement
were adopted and are being realized. The major question now was: 'How
do we keep the interest in quality and customer orientation alive?' Some
of the answers were as follows:

• Installation of a permanent working group for progress monitoring, chaired by the head of the DTP. This group monitored the progress of the five working groups set up to implement concrete solutions to bottlenecks.

- Annual or biannual communication days to discuss experiences with clients.

- Installation of a specific functionary whose daily work, as executive member of the working group on the progress monitoring of quality and customer orientation, included continuity of the activities.

- Explicit incorporation of training courses on quality and customer orientation into the introduction process of new employees.

EVALUATION AND CONCLUSIONS

In this case study we have described how the DTP of the Ahold concern adjusted its working climate and organizational culture based on a technically completed reorganization. In this adjustment, service marketing principles were used. Service marketing naturally shares its main starting point with product marketing: not the product, not the technician, not the company, but the customer and his wishes are the central issues. However, service marketing differs from product marketing in an important respect: personnel and customer determine, in their interaction, the quality of the service.

In the programme developed, quality improvement was projected against the background of the relationship with the customers. Unlike an organizational change for the organization itself, the customer was taken as the starting point and guideline for improving procedures, communication and mutual cooperation. The programme was characterized by the considerable contributions made by company people, supervised by the internal and external consultants. It may be called an inspiring project, which was experienced by the organization as a success.

Technical people learned how they could view their work in a different manner. The importance of sound internal communication and mutual cooperation was acknowledged as an absolute prerequisite for customer-oriented functioning. Because this issue still demanded a lot of attention, the interesting notion emerged to apply the principle of customer orientation also to services which were supplied internally. Against this background a follow-up programme for quality improvement was realized, 'Service through cooperation' (STC), which aimed at improving internal customer relations. Further improvement in relations with external customers will be realized in this way.

In the meantime, the DTP has shifted further in the direction of its customers by means of the decentralization of the department. The DTP now operates locally in each Ahold unit, but has retained a small central support unit. A major part of the department therefore belongs entirely to the Ahold retail business.

Evaluation of the project identified both strong and weak points. The strong points were the organization and planning of the project, the way in which concepts were recognized and brought to life internally. Furthermore, considerable commitment was evoked in the employees. One weak point was that not all bottlenecks which became visible were solved. However, reactions from clients indicate that the department's image at the end of the project was positive.

In addition, at the beginning of the project the customers within the Ahold organization were quite critical of the department. But at the end of the project we established that the DTP provided services to all Ahold units; so the number of customers had not diminished. Nevertheless, it would have been better if a formal attitude survey had been conducted prior to and after the project. However, it was not considered expedient at the start of the project, when its course had not yet been established, to burden customer relations with an attitude survey or general poll.

Overall, in the light of internal and external reactions, the operation may certainly be considered to have been a success.

ACKNOWLEDGEMENT

The author wishes to thank A.J. de Lint, former DTP manager, R. Bergh, head of the Department of Training and Organization, and A. van Gaalen, Personnel Officer of Royal Ahold Inc., for their cooperation and contributions to this case description.

10

Improving the quality of professional work: the ECOS model

GERCO C. EZERMAN

INTRODUCTION

Today, quality is a central issue in nearly every professional organization. Often quality is accompanied by or coupled with concepts such as service, customer orientation, result orientation and effectiveness. And various staff departments in both private and government organizations are busily setting up and implementing projects to improve the quality of their products and services. Integrated quality management, quality circles, internal entrepreneurship, network management, contract management: such project labels are often used.

All sorts of professional service organizations are interested in quality: strongly decentralized, small personnel departments in large companies with divisional structures; decentralized departments of organization in governmental ministries; and research institutes in both private and public sectors. We also include profit organizations such as accounting firms and consulting firms that wish to work on quality. This chapter specifically addresses the question of how to improve the quality of internal staff operations.

WHY QUALITY IMPROVEMENT?

A characteristic of professionals is that they examine their own functioning from time to time. This occurs while working, during reflection on concrete problems, with or without colleagues. Again, after a project is completed, they will evaluate it with the client and ask him to provide suggestions for improvements.

Members of staff attend workshops every now and then, or take (post-) academic courses, in which new ideas and impulses are provided by colleagues and fellow students. If we typify this kind of change in the quality of staff work, the term 'spontaneous improvement' comes to mind. A characteristic of spontaneous change processes is the absence of a project approach that is managed from a power centre. The initiative for improving the quality of work originates in the professional, and he also determines the way in which he works at quality. For example, a person may determine which ideas he selects from a course he has followed, and decide which ideas he is going to apply. And so, by means of spontaneous improvement, a progression unfolds which the professional himself manages and organizes, sometimes in consultation with a colleague or supervisor. Spontaneous quality improvement is a constant for many professionals; it is a challenge to continually test and develop their personal performance.

Sometimes, however, spontaneous quality improvement of the work alone is not enough. Take, for example, the following situation in the training department of a company:

- There is a growing feeling in the department that they are missing the boat. Middle managers take all kinds of initiatives regarding training without consulting the department. One would sooner consult external training bureaux than ask the internal department for help.

- The training department also feels, especially in the informal circuit, that top management and higher echelons aren't too keen on the department. Nothing is said explicitly, but there is an atmosphere of scepticism.

- Furthermore, the trainers in the department feel they are in a rut. One performance evaluation follows another; hundreds of managers have to be processed, and the initial enthusiasm for this course is waning. Even the trainers themselves are increasingly beginning to doubt the effect of the series of courses. Are there any actual changes in the management style of (former) participants?

- And to complete the disaster, the department of training is slowly being drained. Some people find other positions within the company, in the departments of organization or personnel. Others leave the organization. Vacancies are filled slowly.

It is characteristic of this situation that the department of training's existence, its *survival*, is (or may soon be) under discussion. But there are other situations. Recently I encountered a training department in a transport company which was swamped with questions from management. While the trainers were busy implementing current projects, one division requested supervision for quality circles, a second division wanted training programmes concerning customer orientation, and a third middle manager requested workshops on internal entrepreneurship. Furthermore, this training department wished to transform the nature of its work from organizing courses to supervising workshops – in other words, from instruction to supervision. How should this transformation be approached? How could one win over management for this method?

In such a situation too, existential issues play a role, based not on threats but on the new opportunities that present themselves. But it is more common that both threats and opportunities arise simultaneously. At such moments, spontaneous quality improvement is no longer sufficient: a more specific approach is the only way.

This contradictory situation of simultaneously arising opportunities and threats is visible in many organizations. One of my clients, a research institute in the semi-public area, was pressured by static resources on the one hand, and by an obligation to implement autonomy on the other. The department of personnel, which had a good reputation because of its contribution to recession management, was searching for a new identity in a somewhat confused manner, now that the company was doing well again. For specific quality improvement, how would one proceed?

THE ECOS MODEL

Specific change processes start by diagnosing the current situation and formulating a desired situation. Here, staff departments can use the environment/clients/operations/support (ECOS) model (figure 10.1), which summarizes the most important aspects of their functioning. Ishikawa was a major source of inspiration for the development of this model. His universally known diagram, with its perspectives of material, man, method and machine, was developed for analysing the quality of industrial production processes (Ishikawa, 1976). For service organizations, the ECOS model is more adequate.

The central underlying notion is that all elements are essential for quality improvement of professional work, and that management must

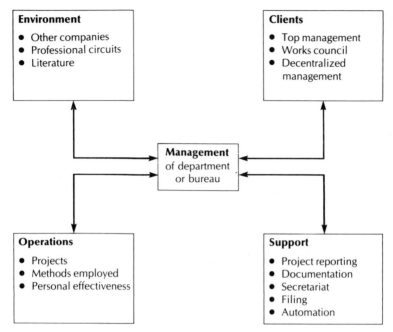

FIGURE 10.1 The ECOS model for quality analysis

take on a coordinating and guiding role. Neglecting one of the elements sooner or later inevitably leads to a department with the characteristics shown in table 10.1.

From this neglect diagnosis we often see staff departments with the following organizational characteristics:

- Division is in functional sections: one section for management development, one for automation training programmes etc.

- Departmental communication is of a primarily managerial nature: determining schedules, discussing whether you always manage a project jointly or alone, progress monitoring.

- Client and (top) management are discussed somewhat condescendingly, as people who don't want anything, who are afraid to stick out their necks.

TABLE 10.1 Consequences of neglecting ECOS elements

Neglecting	Leads to
Environment	Introverted task fulfilment No inspiration from other companies Inventing the wheel again and again Not being able to confront management with alternative methods
Clients	Alienating management Being regarded as a source of costs Image of being soft, complicated etc. Professionals may react against management
Operations	Lack of result-oriented analysis of own work methods No alternatives for own work methods Freezing or even deterioration of personal performance Cooperation with other professionals from a narrow-minded attitude: what is X allowed to do, what is Y allowed to do?
Support	Inadequate use of personnel items such as bulletins, informal meetings: no image building Ignoring productivity increases through new forms of information processing Labour-intensive documentation and filing systems, poor accessibility

FORMULATING THE DESIRED SITUATION

If we turn this bleak picture around 180 degrees, then we can say with the aid of the ECOS model that high-quality professional organizations possess the characteristics shown in table 10.2.

The general picture of a well-functioning department is that of a group of professionals who have an open relationship with their environment and who continually seize new sources of information. Management is involved closely with the work, and this work is seen as a product that is susceptible to cost–benefit analysis. The internal distribution of tasks within the department, and the structure of

TABLE 10.2 Consequences of paying attention to ECOS elements

Attention to	Leads to
Environment	Broad social orientation Input from external environment Learning from others' experiences Attending platforms where professionals meet
Clients	Participating in policy making, preferably at an early stage Thinking about various policy areas together with management: marketing, production, automation Informal attitude towards management But also being able to hold up a mirror to management
Operations	Open and critical discussion of own performance within the department Putting a price tag on own activities Integrated cooperation: the job is essential, not the personal task or expertise Critical audit of own work method, guided by the question: what exactly is the surplus value?
Support	Knowing and consciously managing the department's image within the company Systems to register the effectiveness of own department (creating own profit centre) Information is a permanent concern: 'get behind the computer yourself' Secretaries and administrative support know staff work and are involved

expertise and internal regulations, are subordinate to the wishes and needs of the client; a customer-oriented, outward attitude prevails. The secretariat knows the contents of the work and feels involved. The department regularly organizes workshops in which the work and personal effectiveness of the staff are discussed in an open atmosphere. The management of the department, not necessarily from a specialist background, regards the department as a company within the company, and facilitates internal communication concerning staff performance.

Thus in this desired situation the notion of quality is broadly defined. It refers not only to the actual staff work (operations in the ECOS model) but also to relations with the social and professional environment, with clients and with support. How can the department work towards this desired situation?

SPECIFIC QUALITY CONTROL

One obvious way of improving quality is related to the recruiting, selection and career policy of the department. Via this route a broadening of expertise, a balanced distribution of ages and an adequate mix of juniors and seniors can be attained. A second approach is restructuring departments. At present decentralization and deconcentration processes are taking place in various organizations, aimed at getting staff to function closer to middle management. As indicated before, I do not address these incoming and structural approaches in this contribution; my focus is on culture, on change in the work style.

At the start of such a quality improvement process there is the diagnosis of the strong points and weak points in staff work, for which the ECOS model can be used. Also examined is which of the four elements is least developed and therefore most suitable for improvement. Information about the department's performance can be collected from the client(s), and also from the people working in the department. It would be a good idea to use the Ishikawa quality circle diagram and subsequently link this to Pareto analysis (for more information on these methods see Ishikawa, 1976). One department which applied this method to the quality of staff communication got the result shown in figure 10.2. (See also the literature on quality control circles; the books by Hutchins, 1985 and Mohr and Mohr, 1983 are among the better ones.)

The first step in a specific quality improvement process is to identify the problem and analyse the causes. Subsequent steps are indicated in figure 10.3. Within the framework of this contribution it is not possible to elaborate on every step in this diagram, although each step in change processes produces its own problems. I continue here by providing several suggestions for the second step (generating solutions): on which solutions can staff departments work to improve the quality of their services?

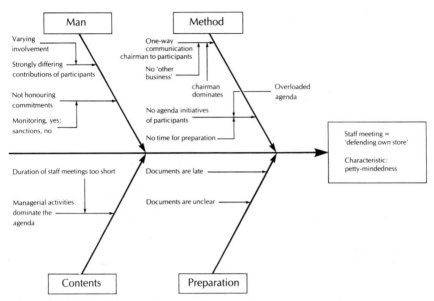

FIGURE 10.2 Ishikawa diagram of low-quality staff communication

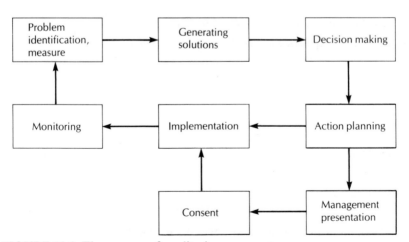

FIGURE 10.3 The process of quality improvement

MEASURES FOR QUALITY IMPROVEMENT

Every department and every bureau can come up with various solutions by means of brainstorming, using the ECOS model if they wish, to improve poor quality. I present several below.

Environment

- Stimulate membership of professional societies.
- Participate in their boards and working groups.
- Maintain diversity in subscriptions (not just magazines).
- Produce publications for (professional) magazines.
- Study literature, e.g. the significance of Pinchot's 'intrapreneuring' (1985) for the work.
- Stimulate part-time positions in universities and training centres.
- Attend courses, appear in external courses.
- Invite guest speakers from academic circles or from other companies to the departmental meetings.
- Create an external advisory council.
- Participate in inter-organizational networks.

Clients

- Hold regular discussions of the work with a panel consisting of middle managers, the chairman of the works council etc.
- Gather information on needs in the organization by means of sounding board groups, brainstorming groups (a marketing technique).
- Invite middle managers to participate in projects.
- Organize pilot projects for top/higher management.
- Interview major clients.

- Ensure that staff work is a regular issue on the agenda in board meetings, and arrange invitations to those meetings.
- Employ an external firm which has easy access to the top.

In my experience it is essential that staff members have at their disposal, or develop, consulting skills. They should be able to make a contribution in the contracting and evaluation of the work which equals that of the client. Also of major importance here is that there is a lot of informal communication between them.

Operations

- Work by quotations, where cost–benefit analyses (both material and intellectual) are attached to the services.
- Ensure multidisciplinary project teams.
- Use a task force (from the client's organization) to design the project and to adjust and evaluate it during implementation.
- Rotate staff from the department per project.
- Compare the work with similar work in other companies or external firms.
- Use flexible programming.
- Make reports frequently and pass them on to the client and colleagues.

Staff members frequently ask how they can assess the effects of the work. I usually refer to van der Hart (1984), who describes three types of effect measurement which organizations and staff departments can use (see also chapter 8 of this book):

Output measurement Duration of projects, man hours per project, number of participants in courses etc.; amount of visible results, for example the number of participants who actually carry out performance evaluations after attending the course.

Opinion measurement Quantified opinions of the clients and top management concerning the (specified) effect.

Result measurement For example, longitudinal measurements in the course's target group: is there any development of mobility in the company after all middle managers have attended the performance evaluation course?

For further elaboration of these types of measurement, see van der Hart (1984). He also states that optimum effect measurement consists of all three types.

Support

- Have an open documentation system in the department, to which every staff member has access and which belongs to nobody.
- Make project reports and put them at the disposal of every colleague.
- Inform the secretariat about the contents of the work; have these (indispensable!) supporters attend departmental and project meetings (partially).
- Deliver the work as effectively as possible; on disk, get behind the computer yourself.
- Publish a staff bulletin for the entire company, or fill a regular feature in the company magazine.
- Involve the secretariat in selecting materials; have secretaries attend a course annually.
- If there is to be a change in accommodation, choose a place as close as possible to the clients and target groups; if necessary, be content with decentralization of the department, or arrange for temporary accommodation at the client's organization.

More and different quality improvements can be thought up for each element in this model; the selection above suffices for this contribution.

We have now arrived at the third and fourth steps in the quality improvement process shown in figure 10.3: decision making and action planning.

SPECIFIC QUALITY CONTROL IN PROFESSIONAL ORGANIZATIONS

A summary of the above is presented here in the form of several starting points for specific quality improvement, and I add a few new points:

1 Specific quality improvement does not replace spontaneous improvement but enhances it. Specific improvement is especially important in the case of existential issues concerning the department. These issues exist both in times of decline and in times of (turbulent) growth.

2 Getting specific quality improvement off the ground is easiest if it is the business of all persons in the company who are involved with the staff department: the department itself, top management and representative consultation. To accomplish this, temporary change structures are developed (workshops, panels, task forces) with the head of staff as the driving force.

3 Specific quality improvement is a systematic activity, in which the process is completed in phases ranging from problem identification to monitoring the implementation. If this process is stopped halfway, the improvement is suspended in good intentions. For example, a professionalization workshop may be organized, but there is no continuation and the results are not embedded in the practice of the work.

4 One element of specific quality improvement is employing a framework, a model, to diagnose staff performance and suggest improvements. This chapter used the ECOS model, but a different model may be just as valuable. Another simple model is made up of the components strategy, structure and culture; I sometimes use it to diagnose the quality of personnel departments (Ezerman, 1985). Whatever model is chosen, specific quality improvement is a broad process which contains a variety of issues. For example, one can work specifically at improving operations, but this quality improvement will not have much effect if the quality of the relationship with clients is poor.

5 The professional nature of staff departments implies that quality improvement processes require joint efforts. An exclusively top–down approach will not be effective here. The trick is to design a change system in which all those involved can participate. In my experience the workshop/task-force/workshop approach is a good alternative. It may contain elements of training, quality circles and strategy development. For the management of staff departments this means integrating available expertise in the department, designing a tight (and exciting) series of part processes and monitoring the implementation of quality improvements.

REFERENCES

Ezerman, G.C. 1985: Personnel management back to the line? (in Dutch). *Personeelsbeleid*, April.

Hutchins, D. 1985: *Quality Circles Handbook*. Marsfield, Mass.: Pitman.

Ishikawa, K. 1976: *Guide to Quality Control*. Tokyo: Asian Productivity Organizations.

Mohr, W.L. and Mohr, H. 1983: *Quality Circles: changing images of people at work*. Reading, Mass.: Addison-Wesley.

Pinchot III, G. 1985: *Intrapreneuring*. New York: Harper and Row.

van der Hart, H.W.C. 1984: *Supplying without Price Signal* (in Dutch). Nuenen.

11

Purchasing as a service centre: the purchasing audit as a management tool

ARJAN J. VAN WEELE

INTRODUCTION

Recently we visited the purchasing department of a medium industrial enterprise. Our respondent was the head of purchasing. He had been recruited several months previously to send a fresh breeze blowing through the department. An important demand made by the board when he was taken on was that he should be capable of improving purchasing results by 5 per cent. To our question as to whether this ambitious goal did not frighten him off, our respondent answered: 'Not at all, because they have no idea how to assess it.'

Those who manage a purchasing department will recognize the problem reflected by this case. Assessment of a purchasing department's performance is a tricky business. The problem is all the more pressing because formulating objectives, planning action and setting norms are generally underdeveloped in purchasing. That, at any rate, is the statement we wish to argue in this contribution.

The importance of process improvement in purchasing departments is recognized more and more. First of all, the quality of the raw materials determines the quality of the finished product to a high degree. Quality problems with purchased components and raw materials not only disturb meticulously prepared production planning and materials requirement planning, but also often lead to disproportionately high costs (which can be regarded directly as waste). For this reason we regard the purchasing function as an important supporting service activity, which creates the conditions for primary industrial processes.

In practice, product quality turns out to be closely connected with process quality. Where the purchasing process of enterprises is less controlled, quality problems regarding purchased products occur increasingly. Product inspection (in the form of incoming inspections and quality inspections) is not sufficient to solve them. A prevention-oriented attitude is necessary, and attention will have to be given to improvement of the purchasing process. From a perspective of quality improvement and preventive maintenance we recommend regular check-ups to determine the quality of the purchasing processes.

In this chapter we will address the way in which such check-ups could be conducted. First of all we focus on the contribution of an effectively operating purchasing function to operational process improvement.

PURCHASING, COST REDUCTION AND TECHNOLOGICAL INNOVATION

Apart from immediate savings on purchasing prices, the purchasing function can also contribute indirectly to the improvement in the company's competitive position. This indirect contribution can take the shape of standardization of the product assortment, reduction of stocks, product and process innovation, reduction of quality costs (costs related to inspection, rejection and repairs) and cutting down on production times. In practice, these indirect contributions often turn out to be more substantial than the amounts saved directly (i.e. exclusively by purchasing).

To give an idea of the way in which purchasing can contribute indirectly to the corporate result, we would mention the following examples:

Product standardization

Purchasing can contribute to cost price reduction by striving for standardization of the product package. Basically this implies that similar products can be bought from various suppliers, which means that purchasing can take advantage of competitive bidding. Furthermore, standardization accomplishes savings, because there is a reduction in the variety of articles which must be kept in stock.

Stock reduction

In the Western interpretation of management, stocks are seen as insurance against scheduling problems (Schonberger, 1982). These problems can result from the difficulty in predicting the outgoing materials flow (sales forecasts are hard to give, or are not made). On the other hand, they may be due to irregularities in the delivery of purchased materials. This kind of scheduling problem is usually absorbed by safety stocks (van Weele, 1984). By imposing a solid discipline on suppliers and enforcing it, and by realizing flexible deliveries, purchasing can contribute to a reduction of the capital tied up in stocks, and in this way accomplish a reduction in costs for the company.

Contribution to innovation

Von Hippel (1978) established that successful industrial innovations often follow from an intensive interaction between suppliers and buyers. To actively pursue this kind of interaction is a task for purchasing. In this way, purchasing can actively contribute to a continuous innovation and improvement of products, which may result in a stronger competitive position in the end market. Other publications also show that the purchasing function can play an initiating role regarding innovation processes (Barreyre, 1976).

Reduction of quality costs

We mentioned earlier that purchasing can contribute to a reduction in quality costs. When products are delivered by suppliers, many companies conduct both an incoming and a quality inspection. Part of purchasing's task is to minimize quality costs in the enterprise, as far as they are related to purchased materials. The costs of incoming and quality inspection of purchased goods can be reduced by selecting suppliers who have their production well under control and who possess a sound quality organization.

Increasing flexibility

Pressured by international competition, more and more companies attempt implementation of flexible production systems. These systems are geared towards improving a company's market responsiveness. Some ways in which attempts are made to accomplish this are striving for improved quality, minimizing stocks and achieving higher turnover rates in production.

Implementation of this kind of system (also known as manufacturing resources planning, KANBAN and just-in-time production) demands a high performance level from suppliers. Purchasing will have to impose these demands on carefully selected suppliers! A purchasing policy which also aims at improving supplier performance will definitely benefit the company's decisiveness in its end markets.

These examples clarify that an effectively functioning purchasing department has some important contributions to make to operational process improvement, apart from improvements in the quality of products. New developments in production control, materials management and product and process innovation make much higher demands on many purchasing departments. Both these demands and their consequences for the organization and personnel of the purchasing department will have to be recognized in time. The purchasing audit can be used to assess the balance between the goals and objectives of the purchasing department on one hand, and its results on the other.

THE PURCHASING AUDIT AS A MANAGEMENT TOOL

The goal of all forms of organizational research is that the organization, or the organizational section which is being researched, benefits from it. Based on observed bottlenecks, measures must be designed which can lead to an improvement in functioning. We regard audits as a special form of organizational research: they are always action oriented, as opposed to more descriptive organizational research. It is therefore justified to expect audit-oriented research to make statements concerning the quality of the functioning of the organizational unit being studied, the possible bottlenecks in this functioning and the measures which could lead to improvement. It is of major importance that management of the unit under audit recognizes itself in both the diagnosis and the proposed direction of development or solution. If this is not the case, implementation of the proposed improvement measures will definitely suffer, and this will result in the continued existence of the observed bottlenecks.

The effectiveness of this kind of organizational research therefore depends not only on the expertise with which the research is conducted, but certainly also on the degree to which support for the improvement measures is created. In all cases this implies that the management of the organizational unit under examination is closely involved in the research, especially in the creative phase when future-oriented improvement measures must be developed. Apart from determining a direction of development, the aim of organizational research therefore is to create sufficient organizational support. Otherwise the chances are that the report will disappear into some drawer, never to be found again. This requires high-quality research.

By means of audit research, attempts are made to form an image of the balance between on the one hand the organization's planned goals and tasks, and on the other the material and intellectual resources available to realize those goals and tasks. The hypothesis is that organizational problems are caused by the existence of an excessive tension between the two. Possible solutions to an imbalance include the following:

1 The level of ambition is adjusted: based on the available resources, some goals and tasks prove impracticable. Part of the solution can then be sought in adjusting the ambitions, on the principle that 'If we can't do what we want, we will simply have to want less.'
2 The resources can be adjusted: based on the premise that the level of ambition must be maintained, resources need to be increased, or the existing resources must be used more effectively. The motto becomes: 'If we can't do what we want, we will just have to obtain more or better means and/or use the existing resources more effectively.'
3 A combination of adjustments to ambition and resources is selected. In many organizational problems, the solution contains elements of both.

Audits can be preventive or curative in nature. *Preventive audits* can be compared with periodical check-ups: with the aid of a limited number of standard checks, the organization is tested to see whether it meets the expectations of its most important stakeholders. *Curative audits* focus on acute problems in the organization's health. The situation can be grave to such a degree that immediate treatment is imperative. Based on a rapid diagnosis, the expert determines the treatment, which is then carried out energetically. This is what is known in organizational circles as turn-around research. After such an operation, the organization often undergoes a substantial metamorphosis. Top management and personnel are reorganized, new managers are recruited, the product assortment is reorganized and so on. This kind of research, analogous to drastic medical operations, must be carried out by experts. The required 'medical' knowledge is often not present internally. More opportunities for self-medication are found in the area of prevention-oriented research. That is where our focus will be in the remaining discussion of this subject.

PROBLEMS AND PITFALLS

The most important problems or pitfalls in assessing the performance of purchasing departments are:

- The absence of an unambiguous goal–means relation
- The absence of measurable goal and tasks
- The impossibility of isolating purchasing department performance from the performance of other departments
- The common resistance to auditing research.

Absence of an unambiguous goal–means relation

In purchasing there is no unambiguous goal–means relation. In other words, there is no immediate connection between the resources of a purchasing department and its results. This is why the development of ratios is so difficult, or even impossible. It is much easier to develop them for technical production processes or production departments, which have far more direct connections between results and means.

In terms of purchasing, this means that it is not possible to derive performance standards for the purchasing department from purchasing departments in other organizations. What can be done is to gather important purchasing data over a number of years, and conduct a time series analysis. This procedure may yield useful insights into shifts in, for example, the department's workload and the available capacity.

Absence of measurable goals and tasks

Where performance standards cannot be derived from the purchasing departments of other organizations, they will have to be derived from the goals, tasks and responsibilities which are assigned to the purchasing department in a specific case. A very important issue here is that these goals must be measurable, or verifiable in terms of realization. In practice, we observe that the formulating of goals and action planning are underdeveloped in purchasing. Where this is so, an objective assessment of the department's performance is not possible. To be able to form an opinion about the performance of the unit under audit, one will have to fall back on the impressions of two groups:

1 Those involved from the department. Very often this produces a distorted image, as the employees will generally give a more positive assessment of their department's performance than the surrounding departments. This result is not limited to purchasing department audits; similar experiences were reported in audits of other departments.

2 The major stakeholders of the department in question. In the case of the purchasing department these stakeholders are:
   (a) The internal users (production planning, research and development, maintenance department, sales department etc.)
   (b) Higher and adjacent management echelons
   (c) Representatives from the supplier market.

The fundamental idea behind this procedure is that the quality of internal service is determined ultimately by the purchasing department's internal customers. Therefore a picture of the purchasing department's performance is obtained by means of in-depth interviews with a limited number of representatives from these groups (see figure 11.1). Assessment of the department's performance becomes increasingly positive as fewer complaints about the departments are heard, and as more positive remarks about the quality of service are made.

Impossibility of isolating purchasing results

Purchasing is located at the end of the information flow and at the beginning of the materials flow. This is not an enviable position. If one

FIGURE 11.1 Audit of the purchasing department: three levels of perception

of the previous links in the materials requirement planning process does not function well, this directly affects the purchasing department's performance. The phenomenon of rush orders, for example, is often caused not by bad purchasing performance but by defective production planning. Rejection problems very often cannot be ascribed solely to suppliers, but are also caused by inadequate specifications from the engineering department. Purchasing results are invariably joint results; the best results are always obtained in close cooperation with other departments. Acknowledgement of this concept implies that a purchasing audit's primary focus is on the interfaces between the purchasing department and other departments, and/or the supplier market.

Resistance to the audit

Organizational audits are not value free. They concern the performance of organizations, and therefore the performance of people. Furthermore, they are aimed at identifying weaknesses in the organization. As such they basically form a threat to every manager; for the duration of the audit they live in a glasshouse. Some managers are better equipped to deal with this than others. The decisive factor in the purchasing manager's attitude is his faith in his board and their faith in him. If the results are interpreted unilaterally by management, the willingness to cooperate will be small. If the board adopts a constructive attitude, this will have a positive impact on the attitude of the purchasing manager or his department. These considerations imply that the purchasing audit is an instrument which must be used sensibly and with great care.

HOW TO CONDUCT A PURCHASING AUDIT

Figure 11.2 can serve as the point of reference for the elements which must be included in a purchasing audit. This figure shows that the final

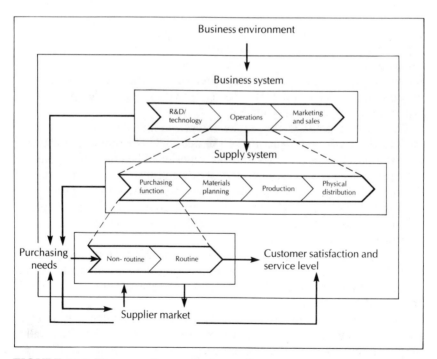

FIGURE 11.2 Elements of a purchasing audit

purchasing results, in the form of customer satisfaction and degree of service, are affected by several factors:

- The requirements that the corporate system lays down for the purchasing function. Purchasing policy must be tuned to overall company policy; changes in the business system will affect purchasing needs or the required performance of the department.

- The demands that the supply system makes on the purchasing function. The purchasing function must react optimally to the wishes of its internal customers. Changes in the supply system manifest themselves in altered purchasing needs. The purchasing department will have to react to these changes or anticipate them flexibly.

- The opportunities provided by the supplier market to fulfil the defined purchasing needs. Changes at the supplier's end or in the supplier market can affect purchasing needs (specific purchasing needs cannot be filled automatically); on the other hand, the suppliers affect internal customer satisfaction.

The purchasing audit will have to map the major requirements that the stakeholders assign to the purchasing department, as well as the changes which occur in these requirements. This implies that the audit must pay attention to the quality of the interfaces between purchasing and other departments. Regarding the internal performance of the purchasing department, a distinction can be made between non-routine purchasing activities (purchasing engineering, purchasing market research, supplier selection etc.) and routine purchasing activities (e.g. order processing, expediting, supplier rating etc.).

The starting point is the intake interview, in which the consultant clarifies the goals and structure of the audit. This is done in a meeting with the purchasing manager and his superior. The consultant gives an indication of what can be expected of the audit, and an explanation of the method. Ideally, this is followed by an introduction to the purchasing department. During this introduction, the purchasing manager explains the functioning of his department. After that, the rest of the organization is informed about the audit.

Subsequently the researchers set to work. First of all they gather factual information concerning the purchasing department with the aid of a structured checklist. Table 11.1 shows several subjects on which data could be gathered.

Then a selection is made of the key personnel to be interviewed. They are representatives of the categories mentioned in table 11.1. Naturally, confidentiality towards the respondents must be guaranteed. This frequently constitutes a reason for using external consultants in the research.

TABLE 11.1 Examples of purchasing key data

Commercial data: sales turnover, cost of materials, ratio of materials cost to sales turnover

Personnel and organization: total number of employees, number of purchasing employees (divided according to educational level, functioning level, years of experience), ratio of purchasing employees to total employees

Purchasing's place in the organization (organizational diagram)

Reporting relationships: top management, materials management etc.

Job description purchasing department: primary tasks, authority and responsibilities of the purchasing department

Actual purchasing data: number of articles (production related, non-production related), number of suppliers, number of purchasing requisitions, number of requests for quotations, number of orders, number of purchasing invoices

Pareto analyses of purchasing turnover according to article, order quantities, supplier, country of origin etc.

Purchasing department budget, divided according to nature of costs

Relations with other departments

Action plans in the areas of cost reduction, quality improvement, automation etc.

Purchasing procedures etc.

One of the problems that manifests itself in a purchasing audit is the structuring of the multitude of data. Based on the mass of factual data gathered, and on the interviews conducted, a recognizable image of the functioning of the purchasing department must be constructed. This research phase is of major importance, as it will serve as a starting point for the improvement measures which are to be formulated.

The method developed by Kempen (1979) is very useful in this respect. In his view, a healthy organization has two chief characteristics:

- It *knows* what it wants to accomplish (formulation of goals).

- It is *capable* of attaining it (realization of goals).

Kempen presents six indicators, with the aid of which statements can be made about the functioning of an organization (see table 11.2). The six indicators can be divided into those related to the formulation of goals, and those related to the realization of goals. In table 11.2 these indicators have been elaborated for the purchasing audit in the form of questions.

The picture obtained in this way is first checked with the purchasing manager. This consultation also provides the opportunity to exchange ideas regarding improvement measures. Then a meeting with top

TABLE 11.2 Qualitative indicators for purchasing audit (adapted from Kempen, 1979)

FORMULATION OF GOALS

Goal orientation
What are the purchasing department's goals?
What are the purchasing department's responsibilities?
To what extent are the purchasing department's tasks known and verifiable in terms of realization?

Outward orientation
Does the purchasing department communicate sufficiently with its internal customers?
Is there adequate reaction to the wishes and desires of the internal customers?
Is the purchasing department sufficiently aware of new developments?

Vulnerability
What are the major break-off risks for the company in the purchasing department's performance?
Have sufficient measures been taken to anticipate these break-off risks?
Has the continuity of purchasing activities been guaranteed sufficiently?

REALIZATION OF GOALS

Steering power
Does the purchasing department realize its tasks?
Is the purchasing department equipped in terms of people and systems to fulfil its tasks?
Are adjustments made on time?

Flexibility
Is the reaction to changing customers' wishes adequate?
Is there sufficient interest in new developments?
Which important changes have taken place in the service and organization of the purchasing department?

Management
Is teamwork within the purchasing department sufficiently developed?
Is the purchasing department a worthy partner for discussion of your problems?
Is the quality of personnel adequate?

management follows. After this meeting a final report is drawn up, which contains recommendations in the form of a policy plan or action programme. An important part of the final report is taken up by the performance indicators, which will serve in future as a means of monitoring process improvement. Although effective performance indicators will differ by company, they must always relate to every element in the purchasing process; therefore, apart from price, they must also address quality, supplier reliability and internal and external lead times. In most cases the actual performance indicators are a selection from the examples given in table 11.3.

PURCHASING AUDIT CASE STUDY

Several years ago, we were involved in the audit of the purchasing department of an internationally operating producer of transport materials. In its strategic policy, this company strove for quality management. For this reason large sums were spent annually on product development and product improvement. A large number of projects was undertaken in this area every year, and this led to a veritable explosion in new components and suppliers. One of the consequences was that the purchasing department's workload had increased by 60 per cent over the past three years, while a 10 per cent decrease in manpower had taken place over the same period. The purchasing director was of the opinion that the pressure brought to bear on his department was becoming intolerable; he felt that expansion of the department was necessary. The high workload furthermore caused a great number of issues to be neglected: there was no time for real purchasing activities, which was why, to his dismay, evident opportunities for cost reduction were ignored. The question was how to communicate to top management the evident imbalance between goals and tasks on one hand, and the limited resources of the purchasing department on the other.

Our analyses confirmed that an imbalance existed between the tasks and responsibilities of the purchasing department on the one hand, and the material and intellectual means on the other. Owing to the changes in development and production – in the form of a growing number of development projects, reduced production times and flexibility – which had taken place in previous years, the demands on the purchasing department's performance increased. This became especially clear in the areas of delivery reliability and quality; on these aspects suppliers did not perform as expected. The opinion was, furthermore, that the purchasing

TABLE 11.3 Examples of performance indicators for purchasing departments

Area	Measurement aimed at	Continuous/ incidental	Examples
Purchased materials prices and costs	Purchased materials cost control	C	Materials budgets, variance reports, price inflation reports, purchasing turnover, purchasing cost saving and avoidances, impact on return on investment
	Purchased materials cost reduction	C	
Quality of purchased materials and services	Early purchasing involvement in design and development	I	Time spent by purchasing on design and engineering projects, initial sampling reject rate (%), reject rate (%), quality costs per supplier
	Incoming inspection quality control and assurance	C	
Purchasing logistics and supply	Monitoring requisitioning	I	Purchasing administrative leadtimes, order backlog (per buyer), rush orders, delivery reliability index per supplier, materials shortages, inventory turnover ratio, just-in-time deliveries
	Delivery reliability (quality and quantity)	C	
Purchasing staff and organization	Training and motivation of purchasing staff	I	Time and workload analysis of purchasing department, purchasing budget, purchasing and supply audit
	Purchasing management quality		
	Purchasing systems and procedures		
	Purchasing research		

department did not anticipate these developments adequately. The buyers were only interested in aspects of price.

Internally, few changes had taken place in the department's organization in recent years; the buyers' pattern of tasks was quite traditional. Apart from making contracts, they were responsible for the follow-up on outstanding orders. A substantial part of the available time was spent on this. The rest was taken up by troubleshooting activities. This is why the activities were for the most part reactive instead of proactive and preventive. In the area of automation, little progress was made, especially in comparison with materials planning and inventory control.

The picture constructed was checked with the steering committee and was completely recognizable. An action programme was designed jointly, containing among others the following ingredients:

- Separation of commercial initial purchasing tasks and administration related tasks, materials planning and control tasks. This was to give the buyers time to concern themselves with commercial purchasing activities.

- Higher priority for improving purchasing computer systems. This was a prerequisite for scoring on the first point. Routine tasks would have to be taken over by the computer. An automation action programme was designed for the next three years, and two systems analysts were assigned full-time to implement this programme.

- Expansion of buyers' tasks in terms of improvements in quality and delivery reliability, to enable purchasing decisions to be based on more aspects than price alone. A so-called 'bottom 20' list was drawn up for every buyer, containing the 20 suppliers with the lowest performance on quality and delivery time. Targets for improvements were established, and frequently relationships with the suppliers in question were terminated.

- Increase of personnel by 10 per cent, and an increase in the education and training budget of 300 per cent. Furthermore, the purchasing director was given the opportunity to recruit MBA students for purchasing positions. This resulted in a substantial improvement in the quality of personnel.

These measures resulted in savings on the purchasing product portfolio of 1 to 2 per cent annually. The corporate result improved Dfl 30 million (£9 million) over a period of three years!

CONCLUSIONS

In view of the importance of a well-functioning purchasing department, we argue in favour of a periodical preventive audit. In this chapter we have compared this form of research to a periodical health check: in a situation of reasonable physical well-being, it is useful to detect hidden defects in time so as to be able to prevent deterioration in the future.

In practice, assessment of the functioning of the purchasing department will frequently have to be based on the impressions of the major stakeholders. Any form of purchasing audit will have to include, apart from those involved from the purchasing department, at least higher management echelons, internal users and suppliers.

Substantial attention will have to be given to creating organizational support. The diagnosis must be recognizable to all persons involved, and both top management and purchasing managers will have to support the policy recommendations. This requires that audits such as these be conducted with expertise and great care.

REFERENCES

Barreyre, P.Y. 1976: La fonction approvisionnement dans la stratégie de l'entreprise. *Revue Française de Gestion*, September/October, 61–7.

Kempen, P.M. 1979: *Business Diagnosis, Alias Management Audit* (in Dutch). Alphen a/d Rijn: Samsom.

Schonberger, R.J. 1982: *Japanese Manufacturing Techniques*. Free Press.

van Weele, A.J. 1984: *Purchasing Control, Performance Measurement and Evaluation of the Industrial Purchasing Function*. Groningen: Wolters-Noordhoff.

von Hippel, E.R. 1978: Successful industrial products from customer ideas. *Journal of Marketing*, January, 39–49.

12

Government organizations and their customers in The Netherlands: strategy, tactics and operations

HEIN W.C. VAN DER HART

INTRODUCTION

Customer orientation can yield an interesting competitive advantage, especially in the industrial service sector. In general, competitive advantages are less relevant to government institutions, because competition is virtually non-existent there. However, in government organizations in The Netherlands there is a growing awareness of the positive and activating effects of the competitive principle. In The Netherlands we see, for example, an increase in the degree of competition between educational institutions. Furthermore, many Dutch government (subsidized) institutions have been privatized recently and so become subject to free competition, as for example the Dutch State Purchasing Bureau. Other Dutch institutions such as the Dutch Employment Offices will be facing this in the future. Building a competitive advantage can considerably facilitate the transition to the free market.

These and other developments explain the topicality of the theme of customer orientation. In summary, we refer to the following developments in The Netherlands in particular:

- Increased attention to the quality aim
- The need for a more businesslike attitude, and the realization that government institutions are also regular businesses

- Assigning managing authority to lower levels, i.e. closer to the citizen

- Privatization of government services

- Application of the direct benefit principle in some government services

- Deregulation: the simplification and streamlining of rules and the existing system of government rules, the debureaucratization of government

- More attention to self-determination within the government.

These are just a few of the developments and trends where the theme of customer orientation plays a central role.

The Netherlands and some other European countries are experiencing an era of withdrawing government, a manifestation of the political desire to leave more and more to private enterprise. However, this withdrawal of government does not imply alienation from the citizen; the exact opposite is intended. There is a paradox in a government with a less obtrusive attitude on the one hand, and a more customer-oriented organization on the other. But even if we descend to the regular daily contact between citizen and government, the topicality of the theme of customer orientation immediately becomes obvious. Officials and departments frequently cannot be reached; letters from citizens are not answered, or only after long delays; and citizens are referred to others time and time again. Especially in this operational area there is much work to be done regarding customer orientation.

WHY IS THERE A LACK OF CUSTOMER ORIENTATION IN GOVERNMENT?

Government organizations have several characteristics which make the concept of customer orientation less simple and less self-evident than it is in industry. Apart from the question 'Who is the customer?' (which is not always easy to answer and which we will address later), several aspects typical of the government world can interfere with customer orientation:

- Government organizations frequently have to take into account more than one target group. Often choices will have to be made.

- It is difficult to translate government tasks into concrete products.

They concern abstract types of service which are hard to transform into recognizable products.

- Government products are not only abstract but frequently unsolicited. Sometimes they are imposed; one could speak of forced consumption. Sometimes they are intended to create the necessary conditions to ensure that certain types of service, for example health care and education, are attainable for everybody irrespective of income. These are often innovative types of service, such as a healthy environment or safety on the streets, for which people are not prepared to pay a market price. We should, however, continually ask ourselves whether these types of innovative government products are ready for the open market, so that the government can withdraw as supplier. This is the case for example with health care and some types of education. Of course, this is a strategic issue.

- Government has its own organizational culture, a culture of rules and laws. That explains why memorandums, texts of law etc. are sometimes formulated in very customer-unfriendly terms. It is imperative that they contain *no* loopholes, and they therefore often leave little room for customer-friendly formulation.

- Government organizations lack the incentives for customer orientation. The government holds monopolies and can force its customers to react. This can easily result in an attitude of 'Customer orientation: why bother?' So the results of customer-oriented functioning will have to be made visible.

- The government official is by nature non-commercial; he is not good at selling his products. That is not a selection criterion. So a natural customer orientation, as in the case of a skilled commercial employee in industry, is not a matter of course.

- For the government, selling policy means providing information. This function could do with a little more appreciation and a higher status in government circles. Apart from that, one cannot rely exclusively on the spokesperson when the issue is selling policy. The policy makers themselves have a major function here. Is the accusing finger not pointed too easily by those in government circles at information and public relations when policy does not live up to its promise?

- Talking about target groups implies that choices are made about which target groups will and which won't be served. This choosing between target groups is characteristic of the freedom of private organizations. Government does not have this freedom of choice and is often expected to serve a diversity of target groups simultaneously.

If a priority is indicated, then this can easily be interpreted as discriminating and undesirable.

- Citizens perceive the government as one organizational unit, as for example General Motors, IBM or British Rail. In reality government shows little internal coordination at its basis, i.e. in direct relations with citizens or companies. It is a large, opaque, colossal organization.

- Government is not accustomed to working in terms of results. The effects of its activities are difficult to measure. Attempts to do this often get bogged down in overly ambitious and academic models. If government results are measured, one often gets trapped in over-exaggerated perfectionism, and the conclusion is 'It's impossible.'

These are the most important bottlenecks to look out for when attempting to give form to customer orientation in government organizations.

WHAT DOES CUSTOMER ORIENTATION MEAN?

One of the things which must be absolutely clear is the significance of the content of the notion of customer orientation. What do we mean when we speak of customer orientation? It goes without saying that it must be more than a slogan; customer orientation must have an actual, practical meaning. Vagueness about this concept evokes doubts as to the value of this principle, which is new to government, and rightly so.

What exactly is customer orientation? The concept has significance on the strategic, the tactical and the operational levels.

Strategic level: where and for whom should government act?

Where should government intervene, adjust or provide services in the long term? Correspondingly, where should government absolutely *not* interfere? Furthermore, suppose that we have a clear image of the course the government organization or the department in question should follow; exactly which different target groups will the government institution be dealing with?

We are talking about a period of five years or more. It is self-evident that long-term policy is of major importance, especially for government.

In this strategic view, customer orientation is located mainly in the aspect of target groups and the nature, needs, lifestyle and other relevant behavioural characteristics of those target groups. In view of the period involved, it is only possible to select general combinations of fields of action and target groups.

Tactical level: how is policy to be sold?

How should government communicate with all the target groups involved? How should it tell them about policy, and which channels should it use to reach them? What kind of effort, concessions and commitment does government intervention require from the target groups involved? In Dutch government organizations, communication (including public information) is very often neglected by government because it has never been recognized as a policy instrument.

Every policy effort should be accompanied by a clear plan of communication. When we talk about customer orientation on a tactical level, truly professional communication policy is a definite part of it. Effectively selling and propagating policy demands appropriate planning and tuning of activities on a tactical level. Thinking in terms of government products is also part of customer orientation on a tactical level. A subsidy scheme is a concrete product, with which control in a certain field is realized. It must be sold as a product or, even better, as a type of service.

Applying marketing principles can be useful for solving issues such as those mentioned above. Using a marketing mix which is tuned to target groups is necessary for effectively realizing government policy. Such a marketing mix offers the government institution the following possibilities for marketing planning and control:

- Adjustment, design of the government product (law, information product or other service products)

- Using or not using the principles of direct benefit and consumer pays

- Adequate mobilization of a network of regional distributors and intermediaries to deliver the government product as close to the target group as possible

- Using an information service, publicity and public relations.

It is clear that information is a very important instrument at this tactical level, but there are other control possibilities.

Operational level: how should the public servant behave?

How does the public servant treat his customers in everyday practice? What are the rules of conduct he has in mind? What happens in the meeting between citizen and public servant? What happens in meetings between departmental officials and municipal officials or educational administrators? How is the telephone in the department managed? What instructions do telephone operators receive? How are questions from the field reacted to? What is the response time? Can the public servant be reached at his desk, and elsewhere? The image of the public servant is built at the operational level.

Overall, in our opinion the question 'What is customer orientation?' can be answered roughly by paying explicit attention to orientation on the relevant target groups at the strategic, tactical and operational levels. Specifically, it involves the following questions:

Strategic Which fields of action and target groups should be covered?

Tactical How should policy be sold?

Operational How should customers be dealt with?

Then a new question arises: 'Who is the customer in government organizations?'

WHO IS THE CUSTOMER?

Customer orientation is a nice motto, but it must be clear who this customer is. In general this won't pose a problem for enterprises. The problem in the private sector is much more: 'Which customers should I direct myself at? Which should I ignore? Which offer the best profit perspectives?' It is an issue of market segmentation. For non-profit organizations in the private sphere, such as the Red Cross and WWF, the question 'Who is the customer?' is also not a big problem. These organizations do not obtain their funds from the customers receiving the actual service.

In the case of government organizations, the customer question is sometimes very difficult, sometimes very clear. In practice, two factors determine this:

1 The degree of direct or indirect contact between the organization and the public
2 The degree to which the customer pays for the service.

The matrix in figure 12.1 reflects this. We can indicate for each quadrant where customer-oriented approaches will find receptive ground.

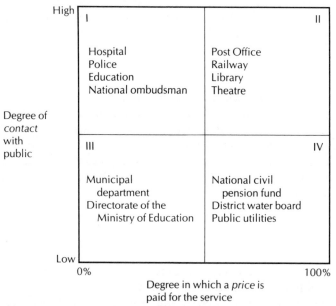

FIGURE 12.1 Customer orientation in government organizations

Quadrant I

This quadrant reflects the type of organization which is in contact with the public, but where introduction of customer orientation demands considerable effort because the public does not have to pay for the services and the organization therefore does not depend directly on customers – at least in the short term – for its continued existence. There is a much stronger orientation towards internal organization. These organizations would prefer the customer to adjust to this situation, instead of having to focus on customer needs in the process of policy making. Examples in this quadrant are hospitals, police forces and educational institutions. The statement 'This hospital is no place for the sick but a place for doctors' illustrates our point perfectly.

Another example is Dutch diplomatic posts abroad. Embassies, and in particular the trade departments of these diplomatic posts abroad, have an important service function for Dutch industry. Company executives are in direct contact with embassy personnel. Therefore it is of major importance that the officials involved in the foreign service know the needs and wishes of companies and can see things from their perspective, i.e. work in a customer-oriented manner. Of course diplomatic service will always remain a typical government task. In view of the related financial independence of customers, it will be more difficult to actually develop a customer-oriented culture in this kind of government organization. It requires explicit attention in the officials' training.

The situation is different in the public health sector, where more and more is heard about the possibilities for commercialization. Ultimately hospitals may become totally dependent on the market, in other words on clients or customers. Then the necessity for customer orientation is felt much more strongly, which makes its implementation much easier – as in commercialized hospitals in the United States. The organization then shifts to quadrant II.

Quadrant II

In this quadrant we find organizations with a large degree of contact with the public, and where customers pay for the service. Examples are the post office, the railways and libraries. These are privatized organizations, or sometimes internal service staff departments which depend on payment by the departments that the services are supplied to. In this quadrant customer orientation is necessary to survive in the long run. This is the boundary between the government sphere and the industrial sphere. All this does not mean that the organizations in quadrant II are textbook examples of customer-oriented bodies. Unfortunately, this is not yet the case. However, here the notion of customer orientation is easier to explain and to pass on.

Quadrant III

Both in quadrant I and in quadrant II the question 'Who is the customer?' is relatively easy to answer. This is not the case in the other quadrants. The most difficult area for customer orientation is quadrant III. This quadrant contains the typical service units within the government, charged with supporting and preparing policy: departments within ministries. Sometimes they work on bills – products of law aimed at a concrete target group – but sometimes their function is less clear. The product is primarily for the responsible minister, and so for politics. The product of law must also be socially practicable and customer friendly. It must be possible to explain and sell the product to the public.

There are contradictions between customer friendliness towards the citizen and customer orientation towards politics. What is the significance of customer orientation for government organizations operating in this area? We have the impression that the organization will orient itself towards the nearest customer; for the organizations in quadrant III this means politics. It is likely that the closer one is to parliament, the less one is oriented towards the citizen as a government customer. But the question remains: 'Who is the customer?' For this type of government organization the question cannot be answered easily, because there is always an area of tension between serving as a legislative customer on the one hand, and serving the legislation target group on the other. A certain equilibrium must be found.

A fundamental reflection on the functions, products and different target groups of the organization can provide clarity and can result in a coherent set of rules of conduct. Regarding quadrant III, an analogy can be discerned with the producer who may make products for a broad target group of consumers, but who leaves the actual selling of the products to other organizations, i.e. retailers. These retailers are the direct customers of the producers, and the producer has no direct contact with the consumers of his products. In the case of the government, the customers would be provincial and municipal authorities acting as intermediaries between citizen and central government. Furthermore, it is possible that one government service provides products for other government services, for example the information service of a department, or the research and documentation department. Some departmental units supply services directly to the minister. In this way, every government service and department – after some analysis – can certainly distinguish one or several target groups to which services are supplied, even when there is no direct contact with the public.

Quadrant IV

This quadrant contains a category of organizations which is somewhat harder to picture: they have no contact with the public, but they are paid directly. An example is the Dutch National Civil Pension Fund, and perhaps (to a lesser extent) certain institutions which collect taxes, premiums or duties, such as district water boards and public utilities.

The flow of money determines policy here. One could say that the organizations in this quadrant are much more money oriented than customer oriented. In fact there are few organizations which receive direct payments from, yet have no contact with, the public. In these cases, the people who pay are not the organizations' customers. Naturally, these organizations do have direct contact with their customers.

RENDERING RESULTS VISIBLE: MEASURING EFFECTIVENESS

In the drive for customer orientation, making visible the results of the government organization's work plays an important part. For if we are able to make visible the extent to which functions for customer groups achieve results, then we will also be able to adjust and adapt these functions more effectively.

In industry, adjustments are made on the basis of customer reaction to prices. In this sector the willingness to pay a certain price is interpreted as an acceptance of the offer. That is why turnover and market share figures are important quantities for control. Government organizations will have to develop forms of measuring effectiveness as an alternative for this price signal. We can distinguish the following categories.

Output measurement Rendering visible the efforts expended in hours or units. Example: the number of brochures produced in an information campaign.

Reach measurement Establishing which part of the intended target groups or user groups is being reached with the service or information. Example: how many people or organizations do we reach with our information and press releases?

Satisfaction or image measurement Investigating the output users' opinion of the organization and its products, in regard to both the practicability and the way and form in which the offer is presented and delivered to the customers. Example: are our brochures clear and accessible? Do we provide sufficient opportunities for the customers to obtain additional information or to react? Are the recommendations innovative, and are adequate solutions provided? Is the report practicable from a political perspective?

Result measurement This type of effectiveness measurement focuses on determining the eventual effect of the efforts expended in terms of the objective. In the hierarchy of effectiveness measurement this is the highest level. At the same time, however, it is the most problematic level because it is very hard to isolate the exact effects of a specific action or measure. In general, therefore, combined effects are measured. Example: measuring the increase in traffic safety as a result of a publicity campaign.

We will now elaborate on one of the four methods for measuring effectiveness listed above: measurement of customer satisfaction.

MEASURING EFFECTIVENESS: AN EXAMPLE

The following is a detailed example of effectiveness measurement in the government sphere. It concerns the service provided by a public transport company. The effectiveness of such a company can be measured according to the *opinion* that the consumers in target groups have of the following product characteristics:

- Travelling time for a certain route
- Extent to which transportation is on time and on schedule
- Price for a ride in the public vehicles
- Service offered by the company
- Comfort of the vehicles
- Frequency of the transportation offer in a certain place.

To determine the effectiveness mentioned above in relation to target group functioning, we need to formulate:

Objective Providing transport for passengers in a certain area.

Target group Population in the area.

Product Bus/tram service.

Measurable product characteristics Speed, price, comfort, reliability.

Transportation performance is divided into components which are clear to the customer and which can be judged separately. We could, for

TABLE 12.1 Example of an assessment card for bus service X

Characteristic	Opinion − − −	− −	−	−/+	+	+ +	+ + +
Speed	Very bad	Bad	Moderate	Sufficient	Good	Very good	Excellent
Price	Very high	High	Fairly high	Reasonable	Low	Very low	Minimal
Comfort	Very bad	Bad	Moderate	Sufficient	Good	Very good	Excellent
Reliability	Very low	Low	Moderate	Sufficient	High	Very high	Perfect

example, present an assessment card (table 12.1) to the customers in the target group area, who could then state their opinion per variable using an ordinal scale division. Based on these opinions, the percentage of appreciation of each characteristic can be determined (table 12.2).

TABLE 12.2 Results of assessment of bus service X

Characteristic	Opinion Scores (%) − − −	− −	−	−/+	+	+ +	+ + +
Speed	10	15	40	30	5	−	−
Price	1	5	10	10	45	20	9
Comfort	5	4	10	15	40	26	−
Reliability	2	6	15	25	30	20	2

Now that an assessment is possible, the organization can also start determining standards or levels of aspiration. But how do we arrive at these standards? We list six possible sources:

- Average of appreciation in the past
- Average of appreciation in similar organizations
- Standards established by the board
- Standards established by a group of experts
- Standards established by a panel of customers

- Standards established by the subsidizer.

As is so often the case, a combination of the possibilities is probably the best solution.

We can express the standard in one figure per characteristic. In this example the following standards, which have been determined in one of the six ways mentioned above, are conceivable. The percentage of satisfied customers for the respective characteristics should be:

Speed 80 per cent of scores $-/+$ or higher.

Price 60 per cent of scores $-/+$ or higher.

Comfort 70 per cent of scores $-/+$ or higher.

Reliability 90 per cent of scores $-/+$ or higher.

Comparison with the actual scores yields table 12.3. We may conclude from this table that the speed of the bus service deserves attention first, followed by the reliability. On the other hand, the users are generally satisfied with the comfort and the price.

TABLE 12.3 Comparison of the standards for various characteristics with their actual values (%)

Characteristic	Standard	Reality	Deviation
Speed	80	35	−45
Price	60	84	+24
Comfort	70	81	+11
Reliability	90	77	−13

The comparison can also be carried out by calculating the median of the frequency division, and using standard medians per characteristic. To calculate the median, numerical scores such as the following must be selected for the opinion scale:

− − −	− −	−	−/+	+	+ +	+ + +
1	2	3	4	5	6	7

After calculation and comparison with the established standard medians, the picture appears as in table 12.4. This method also results in clear priorities concerning adjustment measures.

TABLE 12.4 Comparison of the standard median with the median of the actual values of various characteristics

Characteristic	Standard median	Actual median	Deviation
Speed	5.2	2.6	−2.6
Price	4.0	4.5	+0.5
Comfort	4.2	4.4	+0.2
Reliability	5.5	4.1	−1.4

Which of the two calculating methods is used is relatively unimportant. Practice will show which method is to be preferred. We strongly advise against combining scores on characteristics into a total score; a score for one characteristic should not be added to the score for a totally different characteristic. If you want to know the user's overall opinion, a better way is to let him provide this opinion himself on a separate scale. A measure such as this can also be used to determine the consistency of the answers.

The effectiveness measurement applied above is very simple; in this case the simplicity was deliberate for the purpose of explaining the structure of the method. It goes without saying that the method can be extended by including more product characteristics in the evaluation, and by using other scales.

CUSTOMER ORIENTATION AND EFFECTIVENESS MEASUREMENT

Consciously using one or several types of effectiveness measurement automatically enforces sound identification of target groups. This applies in particular to reach measurement, satisfaction measurement and result measurement. Organizations that explicitly pay attention to these types of measurement will also have an internal climate favourable for customer-oriented methods.

Price as a signal of customer satisfaction and adequate fulfilling of customer needs can then be replaced by one or several of the measurements mentioned above. Figure 12.2, which reflects this, is a variation on the matrix presented earlier. It is clear that searching for effectiveness standards can result in organizations shifting to quadrants II and IV, where it is easier to implement customer orientation.

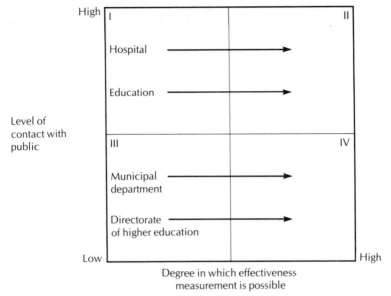

FIGURE 12.2 Customer orientation and effectiveness measurement

CONCLUSIONS

We may conclude that customer orientation in government organizations is a very useful and necessary concept. We are, however, obliged to define clearly the contents of what we have in mind. We will have to indicate exactly whom we are referring to when we talk about the customer.

Government customer orientation affects the strategic level. What role does society expect from the government? Which government intervention is needed and which is not? What kind of personnel does the government need to be able to execute those tasks for the future in a customer-oriented manner? Customer orientation also operates on the tactical level. How can the government sell its policy? How does it reach the target group and with which concrete products? Finally, customer orientation must focus on the operational level. How does the government deal with its customers in everyday business?

Pursuing customer orientation in the government sphere requires taking into account the typical nature of government organizations. These typical characteristics could prove to be bottlenecks in realizing the goals regarding customer orientation. Government organizations that consciously search for standards of effectiveness, by making visible the results of work, will at the same time recognize the necessity of identifying their customers and working in a customer-oriented way; customer orientation and effectiveness measurement are complementary.

FURTHER READING

Hatry, H.P. 1978: The status of productivity measurement in the public sector. *Public Administration Review*, 38(1), 28–33.

Kotler, Ph. and Andreasen, A.R. 1987: *Strategic Marketing for Non Profit Organizations* (3rd edn). Englewood Cliffs: Prentice-Hall.

Lovelock, Chr. H. 1988: *Managing Services: marketing operations and human resources*. Englewood Cliffs: Prentice-Hall.

Permut, S.E. 1981: *Government Marketing*. New York: Praeger.

13

Government as provider of services

GÉ BRAND

INTRODUCTION

Apart from providing regulations, government also provides services. We should be able to speak of a government which is, despite less expenditure, a stimulating partner in society. This is also the background of large operations such as decentralization, deregulation, increased self-determination and privatization. To accomplish this, a cultural change is necessary in which emphasis is shifted from striving for security and 'everything by the book' to customer orientation, a spirit of enterprise and personal responsibility. There will have to be more external orientation, as opposed to internal orientation. This culture change is not isolated from social developments, the most striking of which – apart from technological change – are civil emancipation, increased individualization, the wish to respect privacy and the multicultural nature of our society.

The official (manager) who understands these signs of the times will search for instruments to accomplish the very necessary process of cultural change. One of those instruments might be a workbook concerning task interpretation, customer orientation and quality. To this end, every directorate or service will install a small working group, headed by a pioneering supervisor. The composition of working groups will vary. These groups will report periodically to top management, which in turn discusses the results with the council.

The workbook serves as a guideline for the working groups, who will first consider:

• What is our organization's culture?

- What is our task interpretation?
- Why customer orientation?
- Why customer and quality?

This phase of raising awareness is followed by setting up quality programmes for the various working units, consisting of the following steps:

1 Selecting a quality–customer combination.
2 What do we mean by quality?
3 Who is the customer?
4 What is expected of us?
5 Quality improvement approach.
6 Quantifying quality.
7 Quality agreements.
8 Grounding and scoring the result.

The goal is to make the intended cultural change concrete by joint concentration on customer orientation and quality.

WHAT IS OUR ORGANIZATION'S CULTURE?

Which values are obviously of importance to the council, to management and to the employees? The following list is used to obtain value scores for the three groups:

- Amicable management
- Clear decision making
- Openness
- Recognizable identity
- Inviting presentation
- Courage to delegate
- Direct communication
- Speed
- Eye for essentials
- Political sensitivity

- Increased corporate identity
- Team management
- Internal entrepreneurship
- *Esprit de corps*
- Flexibility
- Personal responsibility
- Creativity
- Friendly objectivity.

All of these cultural traits are expressed in increased quality and customer orientation!

WHAT IS OUR TASK INTERPRETATION?

Task interpretation implies more than just a formal objective. It concerns a choice of values and a clear and convincing concept of principles. Practice has shown that objectives determine the direction of organizational action only when they are emotionally acceptable. A shared task orientation which appeals to the imagination, and for the realization of which one is willing and motivated to apply onself, is an important source of energy. We pose the following questions for our organizational unit:

- What is our key task?
- What do we want to accomplish?
- What do we find important?
- How do we formulate this concisely?

Naturally we already have a known set of tasks and a policy programme. But the issue now is to determine a challenging, meaningful and motivating task for the following period. Formulating such a task orientation requires vision, but also a sense of reality. If one aims too high in relation to the realistic possibilities, it will be a discouraging shot in the dark. And those shots in particular use up most energy.

Inspiring task orientation is based on a growing awareness of objectives and values on the part of council, management and employees. In this sense, task orientation will have to correspond with intelligent observation of relevant developments in the environment. This is also referred to as *mission*. We can only speak of a mission when the officials involved are able to recognize, and agree with, the incorporated values, which also include the values of customer orientation and quality. This requires more than the simple top–down dropping of a strategic cultural change plan.

Especially important is the systematic encouragement of strategic behaviour by the organization's employees; this enables them to respond to every challenge with new solutions which together make up a certain strategy. Inner involvement is the major strength in this process. The strategy which emerges from the floor must be combined with policy planning from the top. This strategic mix of planning by the top and everyday behaviour presupposes joint responsibility and effective communication between council, management and employees.

WHY CUSTOMER ORIENTATION?

The relationship between government and citizen differs fundamentally from the relationship between supplier and customer in the consumer market. Government rarely operates in a market of individual commodities, and the citizen has no freedom of choice between different suppliers.

The welfare state emerged precisely because, over the centuries, private commodities in all kinds of areas were transformed into collective goods. Apparent advantages were seen in a collective solving of individual problems. The solution took shape by way of a collective organization along the lines and regulations of a bureaucracy, irrespective of whether it concerned education, health care, the provision of drinking water, or social security. Furthermore, government in its functions of political and public organization has its own specific task, and will not always be able to comply with the wishes of individual citizens, social organizations or industry. Indeed, the situation is often reversed with a legislative government: citizens and companies are obliged to comply with the wishes of government.

Why do we consciously employ the terms 'customer' and 'customer orientation', which break through government culture? Collectivization and bureaucracy have their disadvantages, which explains the obvious need in certain areas to reduce government intervention and increase debureaucratization. Where the collective facility must be maintained, it may be of value to strive towards a more economical and result-oriented structure and culture. This requires a customer-oriented approach, an orientation beyond the limits of the organization and the work unit.

This development expresses that government is starting to behave more actively as a *partner* in society. For every decision and every service provided by a work unit, a customer or target group can be discerned. The term 'customer' signifies the (internal and external) customers, consumers, target groups or interested parties. Customer orientation does not imply that all the client's wishes or demands are granted; it means approaching and serving the customer in a way which takes into account as much as possible his interests, needs, perspectives and values. The term 'customer' furthermore reflects that government actually consists of a network of work units with a task environment which contains differing combinations of services and target groups. Policy too must be marketed, and the work units (services, departments and bureaux) also provide services for each other. In that sense they are each other's customers.

Internal customer orientation, which is expressed in service, loyalty and collegiality, constitutes a very good start for the active, step-by-step development of an enterprising management culture. This culture change applies to all employees, as well as to the entire organization, and certainly to management and council. So let us start with internal customer orientation!

WHY CUSTOMER AND QUALITY?

Attention to quality at all levels is of major importance for success and for pleasant and effective working conditions. This has been shown clearly in all kinds of organizations, companies and authorities. This is not because we have done so badly up to now, but because we can always do better, particularly if seen from the customer's perspective. That is why it is useful to combine the terms 'customer' and 'quality' consciously, from a new view of changing public administration, and in particular a new view of the role of those authorities, which intend to fulfil more initiating and stimulating tasks. In this sense, quality is the capability of meeting the customers' expectations.

However, quality is more than customer orientation. Quality is more than simply pleasing the client on all fronts. There is also such a thing as quality of content: a sound legal regulation, a technically well-developed instrument, a good plan. Effective design and durability constitute quality too, for something good will last longer. This does not alter the fact that quality is also the capability to comply with expectations, needs and justified demands made by the customer, the client and/or the citizen.

Quality of service is to meet one's commitments on time, and one of the most important ways to accomplish this is through customer orientation, by putting oneself in the customer's position. One of the first steps towards quality improvement is mapping the clientele per working unit. Everyone within the organization should know who his or her customers are, and how they should be handled. Not all wishes can be fulfilled, but it is always possible to specify justified wishes, and to reach clear agreements on these wishes. This can only be realized by making the intended quality measurable, by means of indicators or quality thermometers. Also, a clear, timely and well-reasoned 'no' is evidence of quality orientation and quality.

We may distinguish various areas of quality, such as the quality of policy development and regulation, the quality of projects, the quality of regular service and the quality of individual rendering of services. In the first area the main concerns are cohesion, consistency, legitimacy and effectiveness. In the last, the focus is on courtesy, clarity, accessibility, precision, care and understanding.

Therefore quality improvement is more than a management technique, regardless of how effective it may be. More than anything else, quality is related to attention, care, sensitivity – in a nutshell, to people – and to a conviction that everything we do can be improved upon. The point is to listen more closely to the customer, and not try to convince him that we are in the right. It is a constant aim, a work attitude, a mentality, and as such it is characteristic of a service-oriented organizational culture.

Quality and customer are central concepts for a cultural change which aims at flexible, efficient and result-oriented working conditions, and which is of major importance to the motivation of employees and to working together pleasantly and efficiently.

QUALITY PROGRAMME FOR A WORKING UNIT

In practice, the most effective way is for the work units to make their own plans. To accomplish this, they can take the following steps:

1 Choose a combination of quality area and customer group from the tasks of the department.
2 What is quality to us? What is important to our tasks?
3 Who is our customer? Description of the customer: important characteristics, differences, expectations, complaints.

4 What is expected of us? What are our strong points, our weak points? Locate impediments and threats, and locate possibilities and opportunities.
5 Quality improvement approach. Which strategy? Which conditions, which options?
6 Quantify the quality aimed for, by means of indicators or thermometers. Basis of quality reporting. Start with measuring and improving accessibility, service and speed.
7 Draw up quality agreements, which specify what quality will be accomplished when, for what target group, customer, department or partner.
8 Ground in consultation and procedures, rendering scores visible, celebrating results.

The final stage is programmed integration into total quality for each service.

Step 1: choosing a quality–customer combination

We can discuss quality by first of all determining:

- What are our tasks?

- Who are our customers?

- Which quality requirements are important?

Therefore we must first choose a combination of quality and customer group.

Step 2: what is quality to us?

We can always distinguish the following four quality areas:

- Development of *policy*, such as design of regulations, drawing up of a general plan or a perspective paper.

- Organization and execution of non-recurrent *projects*, although this may take several years, as for example regional plans, the organization of a demonstration or an employment project etc.

- Regular *service*, such as the application of a subsidy scheme, registration of traffic data etc.

- Taking care of *communication*, that is answering letters, distributing information, putting people and institutions in touch with each other, giving out information and presentation etc.

In the various task areas, various quality requirements will be operative and various (groups of) customers may be involved:

Policy development Is policy developed with regard to vision, consistency, cohesion, current affairs, meticulous foundation, weighing of interests, value for the future, legitimacy, involvement, effectiveness and practical applicability – for the council and interested parties? Are the notes and plans clearly structured, systematically founded, concise, clear, readable and on time?

Projects Do the projects have clear objectives and results, project plans and budgets, clear rules, a research strategy and time and cost control – with and for the partners?

Service Is service aimed at legal security and clarity, timeliness, speed, effectiveness, instrumentality and accessibility – by and for interested parties? Can the official in charge be reached?

Communications Are communications understandable, readable, friendly, unambiguous, rapid, concise and empathic – for the individual customer or institution?

Step 3: who is the customer?

Citizens are more than customers! They are the bearers of democracy, the supporters of government. Often they have no choice in suppliers of government services. Political administrators, party members and members of commissions of parliament, council or state are also more than customers. They carry political responsibility. However, both citizen and government are dependent on the *quality* of official service and as such they are customers. Customer orientation is to look beyond the boundaries of one's own work unit to the interests of the customer or the target group.

Internal customer groups include:

- Political leaders, aldermen, delegates, council, committees, commissioner

- Services or directorates

- Departments, auxiliary services, bureaux
- Colleagues, employees and managers.

External customer groups comprise:

- Government, provinces and/or municipalities
- Other authorities and district water boards
- Industry, organizations
- Social groups, pressure groups
- Citizens.

The quality improvement area can now be chosen as a combination of one of these customer groups and one of the four quality areas of policy, projects, service and communication, as in table 13.1.

Step 4: what is expected of us?

To ascertain what is expected of us, we can ask the following:

- Which five points in our organization are strong in relation to the chosen quality area and seen from the customers' point of view? And which five are weak?
- Which five developments in this area are favourable to quality improvement? And which five impede it?
- What are the customers' expectations?
- Where are the best opportunities for improving quality?
- How can we obtain commitment from colleagues?

Step 5: quality improvement approach

- Which is the most important quality problem?
- Where are the causes (figure 13.1)?
- What are the results of the 80/20 (Pareto) analysis?

TABLE 13.1

Quality areas	Internal customer groups				External customer groups				
	Political leaders or directorates	Other departments	Auxiliary services	Colleagues	Municipalities or provinces	Other authorities	Industry	Social groups	Citizens
Policy									
Projects									
Regular service									
Communications									

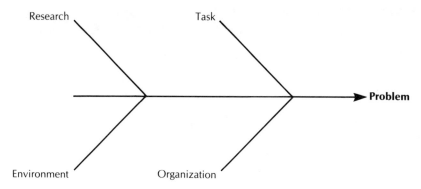

FIGURE 13.1

- Which solutions and options (see below) do we apply?
- Where can we get quick results?

The following options might be applied:

- Use a public panel.
- Give presentation training.
- Provide language training for improved clarity.
- Clean up forms and letters.
- Reduce production times.
- Determine decision periods.
- Increase accessibility.
- Make an inventory of customers and needs.
- Set up customer contact registration.
- Register complaints and questionnaires.
- Draw up a marketing plan for service.
- Improve information and instruction.
- Involve customers in workshops.
- Organize an open day for interested parties.
- Welcome new companies.
- Signpost, including telephone.

- Review opening hours.
- Make agenda known.
- Lay down operating instructions for telephone.

Step 6: quantify the quality aimed for

Choose from the following list of thermometers – or others like them, as long as they are measurable.

Accessibility

- Number of times accessible and not accessible
- How often phone is not answered and customer is not put through
- Waiting periods on telephone, at desks
- Direct line number known or not known
- Room number and agendas known or not known
- Number of times absent without notice or late
- Quality of waiting areas
- Parking space for customers
- Clear signposting
- Signposting in phone book and on building.

Speed

- Number of reports on time and not on time
- Production time of reports and procedures
- Number of days spent
- Number of letters and applications processed
- Reply to letters after how many days
- Time per phase, overruns

- Length of decision period
- Exceeding legal period.

Acts of service

- Number of agreements kept and not kept
- Number of times of appropriate and inappropriate advice
- Number of times of 'that is not my department'
- Number of referrals
- Date of last visit to municipal hall?
- Exceeding costs, budget
- Number of bills not paid per period
- Absenteeism per work unit
- Annual number of training days per employee
- Number of performance evaluations executed and not executed
- How many times you yourself as manager got in touch with anyone, checked the files, handled a complaint
- How many times a concrete goal was reached
- How many times 'you are doing that well' was said.

Step 7: drawing up quality agreements

A quality agreement is a challenge to reach a clear and motivating result in a certain period. The following questions should be asked:

- For which quality area and customer group is the agreement?
- What is the agreement to achieve?
- When?
- How will the result be measured?
- Who will be involved?
- What standards will now be applied?
- How will the agreement be monitored?

Step 8: grounding of quality improvement, scoring and celebrating results

The following questions are appropriate:

- What consultation is required?
- How are thermometers to be used for departmental reports?
- How should scores be recorded, and with whom should results be exchanged?
- Which scores should be used for which performance evaluations?
- What should be included in management training and modules?
- What should be checked with whom?

Learn from interesting mistakes; do not defend; and do not pass the buck! When the quality agreement is met, celebrate, reward and start again! Gradually integrate the projects towards the ultimate goal: total quality.

14

Quality improvement in a research institute: a case study in the not-for-profit sector

PAUL P. KLOOSTERBOER

INTRODUCTION

In 1984 a large research institute started experimenting with quality improvement. This took place under far from ideal conditions. The institute had not existed very long, originating in a merger between three research institutions which had been operating separately. The institute therefore had to contend with all kinds of vicissitudes related to the merger, such as problems with accommodation, differing company cultures and reallocation of personnel.

The current opinion on quality was grafted on to carrying out activities at a high scientific level. Service aspects and the practical value of the products were not considered of paramount importance. The organization was managed in a strict, scientifically oriented way. Against this background, one of the general managers initiated an experiment with several quality circles.

Today, some years later, everybody in the institute is familiar with a conception of quality based both on science and on customer orientation of results. Nearly all units (laboratories and departments) have experienced quality programmes, either individually or corporately. There have been training programmes on quality improvement. Quality is a frequently recurring subject during presentations, regular consultations and meetings between the participants of quality programmes. A quality steering committee has been installed, chaired by one of the general managers of the institute, which coordinates all quality programmes in the subareas.

This chapter aims to describe how, within a few years, a substantial quality programme has grown from a few seeds planted in initially not very fertile soil. The main focus will be on the question of which factors were critical during the process of development. Two models described elsewhere in this volume (see chapters 2 and 19) will serve as stepping-stones for this analysis:

- Stimulating conditions for quality improvement

- Step-by-step strategy for quality improvement.

The essence of the first model is that a strong autonomy of work units and individuals, combined with a strong mutual dependence, is beneficial for quality improvement. The second model contains the three essential steps in setting up a quality programme and lists the necessary support for each step. For the sake of a comprehensive evaluation of the quality programme in this chapter, the two models have been joined together as in figure 14.1.

The next section contains a short description of the institute and some background information. We then describe the starting phase of the

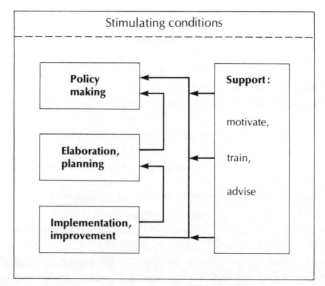

FIGURE 14.1 Model of analysis evaluation quality programme

quality improvement programme in the institute. Next we outline the second phase, in which a more thematic approach is discernible. Then we indicate the way in which the different quality projects are integrated at present. We discuss the key factors in the development of the current quality programme in the institute. The conclusions place the analysed factors in their interrelated context.

ORGANIZATION AND BACKGROUND OF THE RESEARCH INSTITUTE

The customers of the institute are the directorates and inspectorates of various ministries. The products of the institute are mainly:

- Information and advice (telephone, letter, document)
- Results of analyses
- Reports
- Publications
- Technological products (chemical and biological preparations).

The institute is organized in three main sectors and several central service departments. One of the main sectors carries out research into factors which affect human health. In the second, attention is focused on research into the condition of the environment. The third combines both subjects.

At the time the institute started on quality improvement, it faced a number of other challenges:

- It had to cope with the consequences of the merger. Both the integration of the partly diverging, partly overlapping scientific expertise, and the creation of a certain degree of internal customer orientation, played an important part. Furthermore, there was a drastic mutation and reallocation of personnel.

- It was participating in a budget-centre experiment. Apart from the introduction of several new control systems, this also involved a process of decentralization.

- It was expected to cooperate in the general contraction of government operations.

- In a context of legal regulations and increasing competitive pressure, it had to introduce quality assurance systems. These systems concerned both the generation of technological products and the execution of laboratory research.

- It wanted to comply with customers' wishes that it increase the applicability of its products, and that it honour the time schedules agreed upon.

THE FIRST EXPERIMENTS WITH QUALITY IMPROVEMENT

At the end of 1984, one of the general managers took the initiative to install four quality circles. He had already gained some experience in this area in his previous position. The subjects tackled by these quality circles were as follows:

Long-range activity programme (LAP) This quality circle was concerned with why execution of the LAP often deviated so strongly from the planned programme.

Motivation This complicated subject had been reduced to three concrete matters: provision of top–down information; production time of orders; and production time for the material realization of research reports.

Experimental animals How could the number of experimental animals and the number of animal experiments be reduced?

Laboratory X How could the institute accomplish optimum functioning of the laboratory?

Some results achieved by these quality circles were:

- Shorter procedures were devised for the appointment of personnel.

- Improved internal and external tuning was attained in developing project plans.

- The institute's company magazine was used more efficiently for providing information.

- Organizational improvements were made for order procedures.

- The production time of reports was halved.

- The number of experimental animals was reduced by 5 per cent.

- Laboratory X organized a first strategy workshop, in which it was decided to review the internal organization. The changes concerned a transition from a functional arrangement to a matrix structure.

Evaluation with several people involved with these quality circles yielded some interesting conclusions:

1 The very systematic approach of quality circles had a strong appeal. Working in this way was experienced as both thorough and time saving.
2 The strong orientation towards solving problems collectively (especially because of the techniques used) was seen to improve communication between the participants, irrespective of their hierarchical position.
3 The thorough approach and professional manner of reporting (including board presentation) served as an effective lever to increase the chances of success for the recommendations.
4 The long delay in several management decisions concerning more far-reaching recommendations (regarding finances and personnel) heavily tried the patience and confidence of several participants.

THE QUALITY IMPROVEMENT PROGRAMME

After a six-month calm, a quality day was organized in the institute at the start of 1986. Nearly all members of the board and higher management attended presentations by the four quality circles, and considered which quality control issues should be addressed in the future. A few main lines clearly emerged from the countless ideas that were generated. The board decided shortly afterwards to install a steering committee on quality improvement (SQI), which was to stimulate and coordinate quality improvement in the institute along these lines. The main lines distilled from the quality day were categorized as follows:

Quality circles These would be formed and coached to improve the internal production processes.

Testing scientific standards One group would address the development of a method to audit scientific quality.

External products Measuring and improving the (customer) quality of research reports was also a course for quality improvement in the institute. The pilot target group was environmental research reports.

Internal products Quantifying and improving the quality of the central services were the central issues here.

Internal marketing Apart from concrete actions towards quality improvement, it was essential to disseminate the quality philosophy and reach as many employees as possible with the results.

The initial pioneer of the quality circles, one of the general managers, chaired the SQI. The steering committee furthermore consisted of members of higher management from the different main sectors and the central services. Each of these coordinated one of the subcategories mentioned above. A project organization had already been installed to construct a quality system for the manufacture of technological products (good manufacturing practices: GMP); this was now coordinated from one of the other main sectors. Finally, the introduction of quality assurance for laboratory research was coordinated from the third main sector. The main issue here was to be able to guarantee that laboratory research was reliable and reconstructible (good laboratory practices: GLP).

The last two main sectors had at their disposal a staff department, manned by several experts in the area of quality assurance systems.

The SQI engaged an external consultant, posted internally on a part-time basis, to support its activities (interim assistant quality improvement: IAQ).

Figure 14.2 reflects the organization of all quality efforts in the institute. Because of the personal involvement of the author, the primary focus in the remainder of this chapter will be on SQI activities.

Some of the results achieved in this period were:

- The realization of advisory reports based on desk research was adjusted as a result of suggestions from an opinion poll conducted among customers.

- Several procedures concerning the services of the technical department were simplified in response to a similar poll.

- Planning overruns were reduced drastically in several laboratories because of continuous quantitative registration of the realization of the planning and because of related analyses of the causes of delays.

- One internally supplying laboratory introduced a system of account management to be able to communicate more clearly and more quickly with customers.

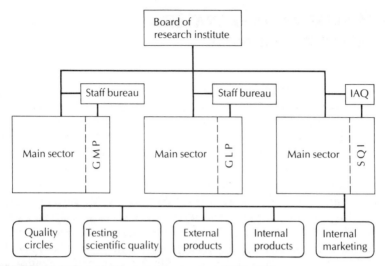

FIGURE 14.2 Organization quality control 1986–1988

- Several laboratories started up a project as a learning model for the systematics of external quality assurance (guidance with regard to content in cooperation with customers).

- An experimental garden (literally) was designed, to beautify the institute's garden with less maintenance.

- Within central services, an exchange course of improvement campaigns and ideas was set up. Apart from that, the service products were mapped at a more strategic level. In some departments this contributed to the drawing up of contracts with customers regarding the content of the work.

- The study group on testing scientific standards developed a testing instrument and an organizational form for scientific auditing.

- A series of quality measurements of the environmental research (questionnaires, productivity measurements) led to campaign programmes for each laboratory to improve the timeliness and customer orientation of the reports. Examples were project management training and improved tuning procedures with customers.

TOWARDS AN INTEGRATED QUALITY PROGRAMME

In the summer of 1988 the chairman of the SQI announced that he was going to leave the institute to take up a position elsewhere. Within the organization this led to a somewhat cautious attitude concerning the continuation of the quality improvement programme and the current quality campaigns. Now and then SQI members were absent from the meetings of the steering committee. Several running campaigns arrived at an impasse, and starting up new campaigns was not very successful. The interim assistant felt he was slowly slipping into an isolated position, despite his regular presence. He organized a series of interviews with the members of the SQI and the board members of the institute before the actual departure of the SQI chairman. From these talks it became clear that there was a willingness to fill the gap in the quality area which the departing managing director would leave behind. The SQI chairmanship was turned over to the managing director of an adjoining main sector.

In November 1988 a meeting took place between the SQI members (including the new chairman), the heads of the staff departments in the area of quality, and the IAQ. The subject of this meeting was the future of quality improvement in the institute. The main conclusion was that the current fragmentation of quality campaigns should be replaced by a high degree of integration. The uniting theme for quality improvement in the institute in 1989 became internal customer consciousness. The first shoot of this tree is the current preparation of a large-scale programme of management training.

CRITICAL FACTORS DURING THE DEVELOPMENT OF THE QUALITY PROGRAMME

Both the stimulating and the impeding factors regarding the realization of the institute's integrated quality programme are addressed at some length in this section. The point of departure for this evaluation is the framework of analysis described in the introduction (figure 14.1). Table 14.1 groups the factors to be discussed according to this framework.

TABLE 14.1 Key factors during the development of the quality programme

Impeding factors	Stimulating factors
Organizational conditions	*Organizational conditions*
Merger and reorganization vissicitudes	External pressure towards quality improvement
Structuring in disciplines	Autonomous units
Weak bond with customers	
Policy making	*Policy making*
Insufficient management discussion on quality	Policy guided bottom up
Elaboration, planning	*Elaboration, planning*
Little line responsibility regarding quality improvement	Thematic programming
More change processes simultaneously	Quantify quality
Inadequate/unclear personal advancement opportunities	
Implementation	*Implementation*
Establish quality indicators top down	Pioneer in top management
Slow decision making regarding quality recommendations	Organize customer involvement
	Exploit deadlocks
Support	*Support*
Steering committee instead of service group	Organize internal involvement and learning moments
	Internal marketing

Impeding factors for quality improvement

Organizational conditions

Merger and reorganization vicissitudes If there is uncertainty about fundamental issues such as job security, job description or working relations, it becomes practically impossible to simultaneously release energy in the participants for quality improvement, which appeals to higher needs for self-development.

Structuring in disciplines In some places the organization of research in the institute was structured around the different disciplines. In other cases a choice was made to structure the organization around the interdisciplinary end products of research. Moreover, a number of hybrids existed in the form of matrix structures. It turned out that in the units structured according to discipline, it was more difficult to focus attention on the wishes and needs of the customers. Involvement with the progress of one's own discipline often proved larger than involvement with serving the customer, because the responsibility for the end product was shared with other departments.

Weak bond with the customer Following from the previous point, it is remarkable that enthusiasm regarding quality improvement is closely related to the intensity of communication with customers.

Policy making

Insufficient management discussion of quality Although there was total agreement from the entire board of directors regarding the start of the first quality campaigns in 1984, this did not mean that all board members awarded it equal priority. Agreement on this subject only grew with time. In the meantime, all this had several consequences: there was no uniform notion in higher management as to the definition of quality, and consequently the same applied further down in the organization; unequal priorities had been established for quality improvement; and every manager had his own quality hobby-horse (GMP, GLP, SQI).

Elaboration, planning

Little line responsibility regarding quality improvement For a long time, quality improvement remained a non-committal matter for enthusiasts. Leaders were not held responsible for initiating quality improvement in their units. Thus many of them sat back to see how their more enterprising colleagues fared before undertaking any action. This in turn caused a decreasing willingness on the part of several early adopters to stick out their necks any longer for quality improvement.

More change processes simultaneously As described earlier, quality improvement was not the only organizational change the institute faced. Other tasks were the introduction of budget centres, the contraction of operations, the integration of cultures and scientific expertise, and the strengthening of the management function. In practice, all of these change processes had to be carried by a limited number of officials from higher and middle management. A logical effect was that these managers selected a few tasks from this multitude, based on strategic or personal considerations (see also the next factor).

Inadequate/unclear opportunities for personal advancement Taking up quality improvement nearly always entails personal risks for those involved.

Will it work? How does the top (really) feel about it? In the institute, insufficient explicit rewarding of quality actions, in the form of personal attention from the top or of little extras (such as training opportunities, increments, and the introduction of quality efforts as an evaluation factor), had an implicitly impeding effect on taking initiatives towards quality improvement.

Implementation

Establish quality indicators from the top down Efforts to establish and introduce one or more indicators from the top down for similar units all foundered. The step of actively considering – and developing – quality indicators turned out to be a prerequisite for learning to work with them.

Slow decision making regarding quality recommendations We mentioned above that in some cases there was a long period between recommendations made by quality circles and the management response. The consequence sometimes was a certain scepticism about being taken seriously as quality circles. Furthermore, a decreasing motivation to remain involved in the implementation was observed.

Support

Steering committee instead of service group The SQI rapidly appointed itself as coordinating and guiding medium. However, what the organization needed in the starting phase was more knowledge concerning possible approaches, advice and support. Instead of rendering services for the benefit of decentralized experiments, the SQI took on the role of central initiator of quality campaigns. In point of fact, the steering committee endeavoured to take the position of the line organization without the necessary mandate.

Stimulating factors for quality improvement

Organizational conditions

External pressure towards quality improvement Apart from the professional and ethical motives of people who display a spontaneous interest in quality, environmental impulses are nearly always involved. In this particular case, this external pressure towards quality improvement originated in four perspectives: the legal obligation to introduce quality assurance (GMP and GLP); developments in other research institutions (scientific auditing); initiatives from professional circuits (certification of laboratories); and signals from the customers (timeliness, applicability).

Autonomous units The control units (laboratories and departments) in this institute had a relatively high degree of autonomy with regard to the choice of products and services. Furthermore, the nature of the (research) work brought with it a high degree of executive independence. This in turn led to a strong awareness of personal responsibility for the quality of the work.

Policy making

Policy guided from the bottom up At present, the quality efforts are guided along the following lines: credibility (scientific standards and independence); reliability (GMP and GLP); and customer orientation (applicability and timeliness). The strength of these three courses lies in their emergence from the initiatives and discussions with regard to quality within the organization. Failure to organize this discussion at an early stage led to a delay, but also deepened it when it did take place.

Elaboration, planning

Thematic programming Dividing the quality programme into subcategories in the SQI was clearly a stimulating condition in the second phase. In this way every member of the steering committee was responsible for formulating and realizing goals in his own category. Monitoring progress was an important item on the agenda of all SQI meetings. Programming actually served as a policy framework for quality improvement.

Quantify quality Rendering the quality of products and processes visible and measurable was seen to have a clarifying effect in three ways. First, the development of measuring instruments led to a discussion about who determined quality, and therefore who were the customers. Secondly, the results of measurements increased the consensus about the nature and the intensity of the quality problem. And thirdly, quantifying the improvements was a strong motivating force for those involved, and very convincing for outsiders.

Implementation

Pioneer in top management The arrival of a new general manager in 1984, who was enthusiastic about quality improvement and who possessed great perseverance, led to a breakthrough. The first experimental quality circles got off the ground. Further rejuvenation of the board led to extra latitude for quality campaigns.

Organize customer involvement Where internal or external customer information was gathered as part of quality campaigns, important steps towards quality improvement were also taken. The leverage function of customer information turned out to be strongest when the information was gathered by the producers themselves, when there was verbal communication with the customer (put down in writing!), and when the information was also quantified.

Exploit deadlocks In some respects this quality programme did not differ greatly from other organizational innovation programmes. There were several periods of calm, of decreasing energy level and increasing resistance. Still, signals such as cancelling appointments, not showing up at meetings, difficulty in getting new campaigns off the ground and postponing decisions can also be incentives towards a fundamental reorientation regarding a quality campaign. These processes took place both at project level and at programme level. A precondition for a positive outcome of such deadlocks was to organize open discussion by those directly involved and those responsible, instead of trying to deny them or cover them up. Getting through these critical moments successfully led to a deepening of the innovation process. Orientation shifted from a few fast superficial successes to more fundamental changes in system and culture. An example can be seen in the management training courses which are being developed at present.

Support

Organize internal involvement and learning moments From the start there were moments when middle management in particular could toy with the concepts and methods of quality improvement in a relatively free and open atmosphere. Sometimes this took the form of a large quality workshop. Sometimes there were presentations with regard to the results of quality campaigns, followed by informal discussions. The opportunity for discussion was also given in every training course. The supervisors of quality circles exchanged experiences in supervisor meetings. Finally, there were all kinds of start-up workshops which contained moments for brainstorming and discussion.

Internal marketing During the workshops and presentations mentioned above, a lot of attention was given to the announcement of improvement results. Publicity was also increased by means of folders, articles in the company magazine and verbal communication. As it turned out, the concrete results of quality campaigns appealed much more strongly to people than pep talks, and stimulated them to started their own quality actions. This is why boosts such as gimmicks were not employed here.

CONCLUSIONS

There are two salient features in the process of quality improvement in this research institute. The first is that the logical steps of policy making and elaboration, followed by planning and implementation, took place in the reverse order. The institute started with the installation of several quality circles. Then a steering committee was formed to elaborate and plan new campaigns. And finally, a coherent and directional policy was formulated only recently, based on spontaneous discussions about quality.

In all probability, a different course would not have been possible in this case. Such a short time after the merger, an *ad hoc* experiment with quality improvement was the only attainable step. This does not mean that the original theory of quality implementation was wrong. It proves, however, that under dynamic and unstable circumstances in an organization the trial-and-error way may be more effective than the strategic way of implementing quality.

Secondly, the institute has displayed a strong tenacity in working on quality improvement. Despite the deadlocks, disappointments and conflicts which invariably accompany such a process of change, this has never led to demoralization. Again and again new ways have been found to work on quality. Perhaps the most important factors which enabled the institute to achieve the present cultural innovation are to be found in this capacity and the willingness to search and learn.

PART IV

Motivation and improved cooperation

15

Motivating for quality: involving personnel in quality improvement

PIETERJAN VAN DELDEN

INTRODUCTION

Each month, the employees of a Rotterdam transport and haulage company receive two computer printouts: a salary slip and a personal product printout. The latter shows the employee's productivity in terms of transport volume, and the number of mistakes made each day and on each trip. The computer links error messages and returns from customers to the personnel number. The company does not use this information in any other way; the monthly individual distribution itself is apparently sufficient. Most people find the information interesting, and some of them even compare the figures with those of others. The number of mistakes and returns decreases – and that is the object of the exercise. Only one persistent problem remains: absenteeism simply will not go down.

So information technology does not solve the whole problem.

PROMISING MANAGEMENT TECHNIQUES

In recent years quality control in industry has evolved from a boring inspection function into a promising management technique. The so-called quality circles which drifted over from Japan have only been moderately successful, but in their wake the quality theme has produced all kinds of new approaches and methods, and these are attracting more and more attention. It is estimated that at present about 2000 organizations in The Netherlands are radically at work with quality improvement. A survey in industry conducted by the Netherlands Institute for Statistics shows that within a one-year period 60 to 70 per cent of companies have started to pay more attention to quality policy and product specifications.

Yet the limits of the original vigour are becoming visible. The Project Group for National Quality Improvement of the Ministry of Economic Affairs reported that only 'a thin layer of some 2 to 3 per cent of industry applies complete quality control'. Too few Dutch companies rise above the average. The Project Group noted that 'in many companies, the quality actions which were started enthusiastically threaten to get bogged down or seriously delayed.' Management is quick to give priority to short-term problems over quality control. Pressure from customers sees to it that attention is paid to procedural elements such as testing, release procedures and the description of responsibilities. But radical structural and cultural changes soon vanish from the range of vision, and quality campaigns frequently end in an anticlimax.

EVERYDAY BOTTLENECKS

What makes quality so difficult? It is patently a subject which one simply cannot be against, and so it should be able to rely on broad approval. In fact, this approval and interest are increasing rapidly. Several investigations show that 80 to 90 per cent of managers and employees declare that they understand the importance of quality. The larger industrial companies have taken the lead in the area of quality programmes, and the smaller production companies and service organizations are taking their first steps on the quality path.

However, especially during those first steps towards quality improvement in the service industries, problems occur. It is often the day-to-day common bottlenecks which cut through the quality drive. For example, for many months an accountancy firm experimented with introducing standards for servicing clients, especially in connection with rapid reaction to telephone calls and letters. During the experiment, one group would cooperate cheerfully while their colleagues in an adjacent department remained testy and uninterested. Two weeks later, the situation could be quite the reverse. The cause was that work pressure shifted strongly owing to changing situations with various customer groups. The resulting stress differed per product and also per market sector, which explained the yo-yo reactions in the motivation of the various work groups.

Quality is only credible as a slogan if your production process is reasonably under control; for if it isn't, you will certainly trip up and stumble. This frequently poses an extra problem when quality improvement coincides with the introduction of new technology. Quality projects then often suffer from the well-known automation diseases such as continuing defects in software, unforeseen adjustment problems, or employees who are not really involved. For example, the management of a hospital decided to make the introduction of computer-controlled planning and patient registration the cornerstone of their quality policy, with a permanent accompanying information file for each patient from admittance to departure as the long-term goal. The details of registration and rostering of duties were now in the software and no longer in the heads and hands of the employees. The result was a silent battle for power between administrative personnel and nursing staff on the one hand, and department heads and programmers on the other. The quality of service supplied did in fact increase, but so did its vulnerability – in particular during the period when the new software was introduced. Sickness of programmers or quarrels within a department soon resulted in delays and in long and difficult discussions. All in all, quality remained dependent on cooperation between people, and disturbances in that cooperation were crippling. 'High tech' without 'high touch' is seldom successful.

PINCER MOVEMENT FOR MIDDLE MANAGEMENT

A common obstruction in any quality action is middle management. Top management reads a book, attends a seminar and hears success stories, or gets restless on hearing pronouncements from competitors about intended quality leaps. Something must be done. So a strategic plan is drawn up, a quality mission is formulated, and a project manager is brought in to implement the plan. The decision is then often taken to inform the entire personnel. AKZO Chemicals put up a marquee in the grounds and held large-scale briefings for thousands. KLM invented a method that lives its own life at present under the name 'hangar meeting': gather all the employees in a large place which exudes the company atmosphere (a canteen or a work hall will also do); emphasize the absolute necessity for quality as a survival factor in a few blazing but cleverly subtle speeches; and give each employee the opportunity to express his or her agreement with the quality programme by putting a signature on a great big notice visible to all (KLM used a pyramid, several metres high, which could be written on). This approach can be refreshing and inspiring, but in practice it usually leads to problems. It creates the impression that the company will shake off old ways and thoughts at high speed, and will quickly put an end to slipshod methods, clumsy improvisations, and those little boundary conflicts which raise their heads in every organization once in a while. These usually turn out to be persistent.

The pincer movement in relation to middle management is especially risky. New policies from the top and increasing expectations from the bottom of the organization usually ask too much of those who must balance these forces. After a hangar meeting the need swiftly arises to become practical, and successes are expected. These are only possible if clear priorities have been laid down, and the instruments to achieve them are available.

A successful example was given by a large travel agency. Middle management and personnel were trained early to use quality techniques: measuring deviations, discussing them in a group of employees with their own manager, and experimenting with possible solutions. This group was also given the opportunity to make suggestions for changing administrative procedures. The crucial point here is that these proposals are seriously looked at during a management presentation. Once they have been stated and recorded, the proposals are no longer informal. Management is at least obliged to present a well-founded reaction. It took years to arrive at this way of working. It is important here that first an extensive training programme was executed throughout the company: directors first, then middle management, and finally operational personnel in so far as they would be faced with the quality programme in the near future. The result in this case was that the managers already knew more or less how to lead a quality group before their employees were informed. Graduality was the motto, and it saved the company from too large dips in the programme.

In many companies, dips are almost inevitable if middle level bosses do not know how to react to cautious quality suggestions made by their staff, other than to point them in the direction of the patient suggestion box. The crux of the problem here too is that the quality *organization*, control of the production process, is often deficient, and this means that middle management cannot get a grip on the problems (see figure 15.1).

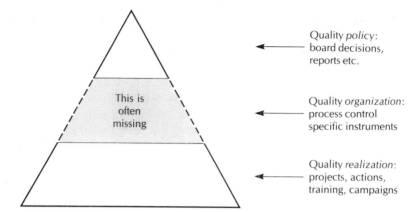

FIGURE 15.1 The importance of middle management in quality improvement

SLOGANEERING

It is remarkable that the pitfalls and problems that occur in many quality actions are not new. Middle management has been subject to pressure for years. Fifteen years ago, worker participation failed due to the lack of formalized support, and also because of middle managers' lack of consultation skills. The temptations and risks of new technologies are well known. One would expect that an ambitious quality programme would take into account the experiences and wisdom of earlier trends and actions. That this does not happen, or rarely does, is probably due to the fact that the concept and content of 'quality of products and services' itself is changing. Various investigations show that a hodge-podge of quality ideas has arisen which are used interchangeably. Sometimes people speak of total quality control if an employee seated at his computer has thought out a quality checklist with which his colleagues can now monitor their mistake percentage weekly. The notion of integral quality responsibility is used too soon, often when the organization has only just started on its first serious project.

Research by the Dutch State Industry Board and the Faculty of Business Administration of the Technical University of Twente shows that even the active companies don't do much more on quality than describe procedures, tasks and quality responsibilities, whether laid down in a quality manual or not. In such cases, quality is like a formal monitoring system aimed at inspection and rectifying mistakes. In the case of public-oriented services, the company is visited by unannounced test clients who have to judge the service provided. Complaints are inventoried, and then either passed on to the guilty department or merely responded to with a polite letter. This is the lowest form of quality control; it is often inefficient because of the gaps in the control net, and with few consequences for the actual service process. The next level of quality control takes a form usually called prevention or process control; it amounts to the work process being so well thought out and put together that ever fewer mistakes occur and costs decrease. Only a quarter of the companies reach this level. This caused the Project Group for National Quality Improvement (mentioned earlier) to arrive at the conclusion that a comprehensive national policy on quality control could result in savings of Dfl 20 billion (£6 billion), because process control can result in a 20 to 25 per cent reduction of costs. But three-quarters of Dutch companies are not ready for it yet.

The third step up the quality ladder is the only one that may be called integral quality control. Only 2 to 6 per cent of companies achieve this. At this level the quality principles are extended to all aspects and levels of the organization. Also emphasized is the responsibility of each person at his or her own work station for the product and service as it finally reaches the customer. External judgement by customers then becomes very important, as does the quality of internal supplier relations. It goes without saying that an integral quality company possesses a refined process control, which means it has successfully taken the first steps.

BUILDING UP LAYER FOR LAYER

Quality is best built up systematically, layer for layer. Experience has shown that this is the most sensible approach. A comparison of Swedish experience with Dutch quality practice indicates that the better reputation that Swedish companies enjoy is largely due to the simple fact that they have been working at quality much longer. In effect, the Swedes approach the subject in about the same way, but they put a heavier accent on training personnel, good and rapid quality information, and the stimulation of new ideas in employees. However, the most important difference is that the Swedes see quality improvement as an evolutionary process. Take for instance the company that has already been working on quality for 15 years, and has still not completely finished implementing the programme. Swedish companies also frequently have their own quality councils, which continuously start up new actions. In general, Western European companies take a short-term view. In many cases, the desire to see rapid results dominates the effort: saving costs, bettering customer relations and improving reputation. This makes it easy to understand why progress stops now and then.

Many companies which hurry to gain quality successes end up with an approach which can be described as a flying start: lots of push, little long-term vision, and often a lack of methodology. They succeed in quickly removing several large quality errors, or rapidly improving some products or services. In the beginning things go well and everybody is impressed with the rapids steps forward. After that, the lack of a systematical approach and policy goals starts to bite and results fail to materialize for long periods. At worst, the project approach ends up as sloganeering: proclaiming the quality message with a great deal of noise and fuss, without laying down a proper foundation.

LATE PAYOFF

What is a good foundation for a quality programme? Most managers have no answer to this question. Sixty per cent feel that more should be done on quality control, but have no idea how. The result is that quality projects often suffer from policy defects. In the first place, they are separate from other policy. Decisions to automate, to reorganize, or to take on another kind of employee are often taken independently of quality initiatives. As a result, quality remains a vulnerable marginal decoration. It is apparently very difficult to keep quality as a central strategic principle when under pressure from competitors, cost increases and new technologies. The payoff can only be pocketed long term, or does not materialize at all because of unexpected problems. The Philips Video 2000 system was technologically superior to VHS, but was no match for the latter's dominance of the market. Quality is not a strategic magic word that can confront all circumstances. Sometimes there is no other way, as in the case of a specialist text bureau which, owing to shortages in the labour market, was forced to have only a few expensive editors in its employ. This caused other functions to be degraded to simple correction work. This meant a drop in the quality of the work which stood in the way of a broad approach to quality.

The latter example also indicates the second defect: a rather awkward approach to employees, who are expected to become more motivated but frequently receive insufficient compensation in the form of quality training, or are unable to measure and inspect things themselves at their own work stations. One mail order company, for instance, has gone so far as to take the future image of teleservice as its standard. In its highly automated operations, the employees work mainly at home using advanced telecommunication and computer equipment; they have almost lost touch with the procedures in the company. This company also works on motivation: it circulates newsletters, and takes on female employees who, because of family commitments, can only work from their own homes. It is indeed possible to largely eliminate the human factor, but that means that the opportunity is lost to develop specific knowledge of customers and their needs.

Companies that choose the human dimension as their angle of approach for a quality programme are very rare, as is shown in the University of Twente's research. In a group of 32 companies, only two put the main accent on cultural change, raising the awareness of personnel, and training. A study done for the Netherlands Industrial Restructuring Agency (NEHEM) established that there is practically no connection between quality management and the quality of work. Working on quality improvement can often mean a broadening of tasks for skilled employees, but for unskilled work it just as often means an increase in the number of procedures and inspections by others. It was seen that there was often a mixture of opposite effects. Fitters at a company which installs central heating, for example, were given the freedom to personally inspect the quality of their work, but at the same time the work planning was tightened up, and professional skills decreased because the company switched from assembly on site to the installation of prefabricated units. Most companies are more or less taken by surprise by this kind of consequence, because thinking about the quality of work is regarded as a luxury activity.

NO STUNTS

As is often the case, the core of the problem is in the start. The trick is to gradually let quality become a self-evident part of the company climate, and to take it out of the game-like atmosphere of stunts and winning trophies.

This was certainly not understood by a semi-government company that decided after several years of quality campaigns to gather all its district managers for a pepping-up day. First a flashy film was shown about the quality performance of the company. Vividly coloured computer animations and fast-cut reports hammered out the same message again and again: better quality is a must, now, later and always, otherwise we won't make it, we won't survive. After seeing the film, the impressed managers were given a questionnaire to fill out: what about our internal quality policy?

The results, processed and made visible by modern technology within an hour, were embarrassing. Three-quarters of middle management expressed the opinion that the employees were not held responsible for their quality. The same number felt that there was no clear quality policy and pointed an accusing finger at top management. The managing director had prepared a pep talk to finish off the meeting, a talk about the encouraging progress of the quality action, but now he had to improvise. His conclusion: the results of the questionnaire should not be taken too literally, for the questions had not been clear and the negative replies illustrated once again the worrying nature of the company's work culture. These pronouncements achieved the opposite effect to what was intended: the audience shrugged its shoulders at these statements and left disappointed. Motivation and involvement usually grow slowly, but they can be lost in one go.

FIVE MOTIVATORS

This chapter has described some of the many ways in which quality actions can suffer shipwreck. The core of the problem is often that it is not possible to make quality improvement a challenge for all employees. Policy, practical and personal aspects all play a part here. Five motivators for quality control are suggested here:

Support initiatives   Good intentions are frequently expressed, but in practice this often leads to separate actions with little coherence. Initiatives coming from employees and departments should also be given *policy priority*, which means that management should effectively encourage and support them by defending and promoting them higher up.

Create a tranquil atmosphere   A quality action will not take root if the ground is not firm. During reorganizations and other major changes, there are other things to think about. If necessary, the start of a quality action should be postponed to ensure sure that there exists the *tranquil atmosphere* required for concentrated action on quality improvement.

Tackle system faults on time   Quality projects often get stuck in superficial orientation. After a while, easily achieved initial successes are exhausted, and further steps are only possible by adjusting systems and revising policies. The necessity of *changing systems*, sometimes a crucial issue for the position of (middle) management, must be recognized.

Organize a broadening of scope   After a few initial successes, it is a long time before there is anything new to report, and interest quickly fades away. It can only be kept alive by broadening the scope of the quality challenge, i.e. by ensuring that everybody regards it as a concrete task. Quality improvement should become *part of the job*, a challenge for each and every employee.

Offer practical means   Quality control can remain too vague. It is therefore important that there are *indicators* which show numerically what level of quality has been achieved. These evaluations should be followed by practical suggestions and work procedures.

16

Five quality improvement stimuli

JEROEN M. DRONTMANN and ARJAN J. KAMPFRAATH

INTRODUCTION

Many service organizations, non-profit organizations and staff departments in large organizations systematically attempt to improve the quality of their products, services and service.

To gain a better understanding of the practice of this improving, the authors conducted a small-scale study during the autumn of 1988. In nine organizations they interviewed managers who under various names function as pioneers in the area of quality policy. The objective of this small-scale study was to obtain insight into the success factors in working on quality improvement in service.

In this chapter we wish to share our experiences, and we will attempt to present a summary of the stimuli in quality programmes. Here we must note that the nine organizations in question were at various stages of quality thought and quality action. One major similarity was that all had outgrown the stage of discussing quality improvement, and as a result they could look back on (the first) practical experiences.

During the interviews our primary focus was on charting those actions which stimulated working on quality improvement. Naturally, the universal validity and applicability of these recommendations must be qualified, if only because of the much heard Agabu principle ('alles ganz anders bei uns': everything is different here, we're unique!).

MOTIVES FOR QUALITY IMPROVEMENT

What were the reasons for starting on quality improvement in the organizations studied? Table 16.1 lists these motives in the form of slogans. A distinction is made between (predominantly) internal motives and (predominantly) external motives.

TABLE 16.1 Motives for quality improvement

Internal	External
We wanted to increase the customer and cost awareness of the employees	Providing top quality will strengthen our competitive power
The internal means of communication were unsatisfactory	The customer increasingly demanded custom products
Shoplifting and vandalism grew to an alarming extent	Our public image (expensive and arrogant)

FIVE STIMULI FOR QUALITY IMPROVEMENT

In the following we will discuss five approaches found by the organizations involved to be stimulating for formulating and implementing quality policy.

Bottom-up communication about quality

Two organizations turned out to have actively used information provided by the employees in formulating their quality policy. The underlying notion was to create maximum support for the quality actions about to be started.

In one organization each employee received a questionnaire, on which suggestions for improvement could be communicated by finishing the following sentence: 'In my position I would like to see the following improvements . . .' From approximately 700 suggestions, three themes were identified and became spearheads of the quality policy. A majority of reactions related to small quality problems and were intended for immediate supervisors.

In another organization, an inventory of small irritations regarding the work, and of possible improvements, also yielded very useful suggestions. When using this approach, it is necessary to communicate the ideas which are launched bottom up correctly to decision-making levels. To give an impression of the type of suggestions produced by this inventory, we present a summary in table 16.2.

One of the dangers of this quality improvement approach is that the expectations of the employees are raised too high. There is a risk in inviting employees to participate in formulating or implementing quality policy by means of questionnaires. For if the managers responsible for quality policy are not able (perhaps for budgetary or manpower reasons) to provide a follow-up (which in the eyes of the employees justifies their efforts), scepticism and distrust are likely to emerge and affect all that follows on the quality path.

Motivating employees regarding quality control in the appropriate manner requires careful action. In chapter 15, van Delden describes five motivators for quality control, which must ensure that quality improvement becomes a challenge for all employees.

TABLE 16.2 Suggestions for improvement

Small quality
Why are there no first names on our calling cards?
We have no name-plates on our doors
Make better use of the cafeteria
Please put a table next to the copier on the second floor
A lot of the time it is so warm in here!
Quicker mail delivery please
Why don't we organize working lunches between departments?
Avoid using abbreviations
Why do we postpone paying our suppliers?

Large quality
Fewer and shorter memos
Meetings to discuss work are a one-way street
Tasks and responsibilities of some departments need clarification
We lack capacity in the shipping department
A time clock could make the hours worked extra visible

Careful structural embedding

Our exploration of nine organizations clearly shows that the quality manager must be familiar with the culture and the balance of power in the organization. In the majority of the organizations examined, the appointed quality manager had been with the company for a considerable period, and as a result had a good appreciation of the company culture.

As a pioneer in the quality area, the quality manager should show his face in the entire organization as much as possible, and in this way inject the quality philosophy. Furthermore, it turned out to be of major importance that the quality manager or quality department was not located at a low level in the organization. As one quality manager put it: 'To get things done, you need power.'

Installing a sounding board group which includes middle managers is an effective way to really integrate quality improvement in the organization. For it enables the quality manager to quickly contact managers who are in a position to deal with quality improvement at a decision-making level. The sounding board group's task is to support the quality manager and to monitor the objectives of the quality policy and the progress of activities.

Balanced internal marketing

The goal of internal marketing of quality is to clarify the policy and approach. It also serves as an instrument to generate enthusiasm in the employees for the policy. To ensure that employees are motivated into contributing to quality improvement, the organizations examined employ a great many 'trimmings'. Examples include logos, videos, films, slides, company magazines, information meetings (in hangar or cafeteria), badges, pep talks by managers, success stories of other companies, brochures, posters, slogans and gimmicks.

When motivating employees for quality actions, it is important for people to see that something is happening. To this end, communication can be used. One of the companies examined employed an unusual means of communication: writing pads. These pads were placed on every employee's desk regularly, and on them the quality items were discussed concisely and clearly. Some examples were:

• Objectives of the quality action and a report of the starting day

- Results of an internal questionnaire regarding image, identity, quality bottlenecks and suggestions for improvement

- Projects concerning improvement of the quality of internal communication, such as meetings to discuss work.

One of the bottlenecks with regard to internal marketing instruments might be found in the relation between the size of the quality action and the peripheral events (the marketing instruments). A torrent of internal marketing accompanied by a lot of noise does not go with a low-profile quality programme. As one of the respondents put it: 'There is not much point in giving the starting shot if the employees are not on their marks.' Based on an analysis of practical experiences, Ezerman (1989) concludes that overselling quality is a notorious pitfall.

Visible quality

Knowing the degree of quality that is delivered can benefit a goal-oriented approach. The results of quality improvement actions are rendered visible regularly with the aid of a limited number of carefully selected indicators. These indicators are meant to illuminate the situation regarding those specifications of the product or service which are most important in determining the quality.

Mastenbroek has formulated several criteria for developing such measuring instruments (see chapter 8). The following examples show how two organizations provided insight into the quality of their service in a creative way.

One of the organizations obtained information relevant to its quality policy from, among other things, external and internal perception evaluations. In an external perception evaluation, customers are asked to give their judgement concerning the quality of service. Many organizations regularly conduct this type of research. In the internal perception evaluation, the far more creative part of this approach, the employees are asked how they feel the customer experiences the service. By comparing the answers of external and internal research, it becomes possible to sharpen the definition of quality and to develop concrete improvement actions.

In a second organization, with more direct customer contacts, the customer questionnaires showed excellent results time and time and again. This caused many employees to sit back contentedly. The energy to do even better evaporated visibly. External research revealed that the validity of the questionnaires left much to be desired. A new questionnaire was developed, which would provide a more reliable picture of the quality experience. For example, this measuring instrument revealed that the customers appreciated a 'sweetly smiling but not technically trained' receptionist, but that they preferred a 'man in overalls' if he was able to assess a defect in a machine and estimate the repair time.

The adage 'to measure is to know' is seen as a reasonable point of departure in most of the organizations we studied. However, in one organization the quantitative approach to quality improvement was overdone. They ended up in an excessive measuring culture ('we measure everything, all the time'), which brought with it unwanted side effects. The emphasis on a quantitative perspective caused other organizational aspects, such as structure, to be neglected.

Integration of quality in personnel management

In one of the organizations we visited for this study, we found a relatively unique approach to quality improvement. In this organization, each employee and his immediate superior draw up a so-called job plan every year, as part of a number of performance plans. The job plan meticulously records the tasks and responsibilities of the employee. It is seen as very important that the task elements agreed upon and the results of the performance are equipped with objectively measurable criteria if possible. This means that the central focus is on the *quality* of each employee's work (his/her products and services). At the end of the job plan period the extent to which the objectives agreed upon have been realized is established jointly with the employee, both qualitatively and quantitatively. Changes in the employee's salary for a new job plan period depend on the measurements regarding the planned objectives and the opinion of a number of internal customers (colleagues in the same or other departments) about the employee's performance.

An example of a job plan for a secretarial employee is shown in table 16.3.

CONCLUSIONS

Taking stock of stimuli in quality improvement processes proves to be constructive when thinking about quality improvement.

The first wave of enthusiasm about quality appears to be spent. Several organizations have been marking time in quality improvement projects, deliberately or not. In others, unwanted stagnation is occurring.

TABLE 16.3 Example of job plan for secretarial employee

Tasks/responsibilities	Standards of assessment
Transcribe, send and file departmental mail	Maximum of two typing errors per document Retrieval time for documents of maximum 5 minutes
Receive, distribute and administrate incoming and outgoing mail	Mail on all desks within 2 days Accurate and perfect registration when assisting in preparation
Keep agendas for three managers and assign priorities	Correct timing; no double engagements Break of 15 minutes between engagements One hour personal time a day
Assist in preparing and transcribing presentations, such as making overhead slides	Feedback from presenter Perfect transcription
Receive internal and external visitors	Happy customer (result customer survey) No complaints

In this contribution our aim has been to describe several approaches which proved fertile in practice. Further investigation of practical experience with quality improvement in the service industry will increase progress in this area.

REFERENCE

Ezerman, G.C. 1989: Three implementation strategies. In G.C. Ezerman and W.F.G. Mastenbroek (eds), *Kwaliteitsverbetering in de dienstverlening*, Kluwer, Deventer.

17

Cooperation as a critical success factor: functional quality and corporate culture

WILLEM F.G. MASTENBROEK

INTRODUCTION

Inadequate functioning of teams, tensions in the hierarchy, disputes over competence and friction between departments and functions can undermine the organization. Excellently organized quality projects sometimes get bogged down, merely because of defective communication and cooperation. All managers are confronted every now and then with problems concerning communication and cooperation. Managing also includes improving the quality of cooperation. Table 17.1 shows cooperative attributes and their opposites.

TABLE 17.1 Important cooperative attributes and opposites

Distrustful	Trustful
Uncommunicative	Open
Rigid	Flexible
Formal	Informal
Cool	Genial
Repetitive	Explorative
Testy	Humorous
More of the same	Open to alternatives
Dominance oriented	Balance oriented

Concepts such as style of cooperation, quality of communication and method of management are interdependent. Together they constitute one of the major elements of corporate culture, because there is an immediate link with the effectiveness of the organization and the motivation of employees.

How can we improve the quality of cooperation? There are several ways to achieve changes:

1 Managers set an example.
2 Existing communication is improved by giving separate attention to the quality of the communication.
3 Training programmes are initiated.

Each of these ways will be discussed briefly. In addition there are several conditions in the area of strategy, structure and information management which affect the quality of cooperation; these are discussed in chapter 2. Finally, several elements for a training programme and some developments in the field of communication skills will be listed.

This chapter provides a very practical description of how improvement can be achieved. Practical also means simple and clear. This may create a false impression, however. Occasionally it may seem that cooperation can be improved rapidly by means of a few simple interventions. Usually it is not as simple as that. Improvement requires time, attention and substantial effort from those involved. Sometimes relationships involving cooperation are in a state of delicate, emotionally charged equilibrium. Utmost care is imperative: this also means maximum clarity about objectives and methods. And that is the focus of this chapter.

TOP MANAGEMENT SETS THE EXAMPLE

One important skill in the field of management has become known as management by walking around (or management by wandering around). This implies that managers show themselves frequently on the workshop floor. They facilitate communication with their employees in all sorts of ways. They aim for informal and personal relationships; they do not avoid contact outside working hours. They show they are approachable; all kinds of formal dividing lines and privileges, such as separate canteens, are abolished. They are interested in suggestions and ideas; they elicit reactions to their own ideas. In short, instead of being determined decision makers, managers become coaches and supervisors of the decision-making process; they focus on collective acceptance and consensus.

The importance of this skill is confirmed time and again. The title of a frequently quoted article in the *Harvard Business Review* is an illustrative example: 'Good managers don't make policy decisions'. In this article Wrapp (1984) states that able managers push through decisions only occasionally: 'They explore, combine and integrate!' In their book *In Search of Excellence* (1982) Peters and Waterman emphasize the importance of this skill. They even considered 'Management by walking around' as an alternative title. A later publication by Peters and Austin (1985) is devoted to this skill, which in their view is most fundamental.

It is interesting to hear what some Western managers, who have worked in Japanese companies for several years, have to say on this issue:

> A person who is a good leader in Japan does not make decisions at all – he finds out what the decision is . . . And because you do not have specialists in Japanese companies, people tend to be more hesitant to make flat-out decisions . . . If the president went ahead without the approval of the groups concerned, he'd be removed in some face-saving way. (*Fortune*, 1987)

Japanese corporate culture utilizes countless other skills in the process of reaching consensus: more time is taken to assimilate ideas. People have more tentative and open opinions instead of presenting explicit and more definite points of view. In general, people try to express themselves with a little more subtlety and nuance. This attitude makes it easier to keep the decision-making process going and to nourish it. In this manner, sufficient support and acceptance can be established more carefully.

The types of conduct described here all have in common that they express a *larger mutual dependence* in the relationship between management and employees.

IMPROVING EXISTING COMMUNICATION

Existing working relations between team members or between departments can be hampered by all kinds of obscurities and irritations. In such cases it may be helpful to take some time out with all concerned to clear the air. In general, regular evaluation of the quality of communication is to be recommended.

Tensions in teams

Team development meetings may focus on instrumental questions. An important aspect here is the exchange of information concerning tasks and duties, and adapting it to one another's views. One way of going about this is to have the participants set down for themselves what they see as the most important elements of their tasks; for instance, the two or three priorities they have set themselves for the coming 12 months.

In addition to what they expect of themselves, they should also list their expectations with regard to the priorities of their team members. Presenting this in easy view of everyone, for instance on wall charts, is the next step. Then a group discussion can help to clarify matters. Discrepancies between a person's own priorities and what his team members expect of him are of special importance. Sometimes priorities have to be adjusted. A number of aids exist to facilitate discussion of team and personal functioning (see the appendix to this chapter). Concise programmes (lasting one or two days) are also available in which impediments to effective cooperation are named and disposed of step by step.

For example, a particular company held a team development conference over an evening, a morning and an afternoon. This was a conference for department heads and their plant manager. The object of the meeting was the bickering about unclear division of tasks (instrumental) and more personal tensions (socio-emotional) among team members. The three sessions covered the following areas:

Task clarification Each participant had about 30 minutes to write down in telegram style on a flip-over board: a short description of his own task; up to three of his own priority activities for the following year; and up to three activities of other departments which he needed. A discussion of each chart followed, primarily on whether mutual expectations were clear on both sides.

Tackling mutual tensions Everyone wrote down in telegram style what behaviour in team members hindered them, and what behaviour helped them to function effectively. Notes were exchanged. All participants gave a summary of the picture they obtained from the notes and could ask questions to clarify it. Colleagues explained and added to what they had written.

Conclusions and solutions Everyone established for himself what his most important conclusions and resolves were. This was exchanged and sometimes amended by suggestions from others. Agreements were made about the follow-up, the primary one being to look through the conclusions together again six months later.

Tensions between groups

Various procedures are available for managing the quality of cooperation between departments, groups and levels. For example, a one-day conference might be devoted to eliminating obstacles to the effective functioning of interdependent organizational units.

In such a conference, the participants will be representatives of departments in an organization between which relations on the job are tense. This may be the top managers, but it is often possible to allow opinion leaders or even entire sections to participate. The maximum number of participants will be around 25. The objectives will be:

- Specifying the most important obstacles to effective functioning of both groups
- Reaching agreements for improvement.

The participants must want to improve the relations between both groups; they must be willing to work actively on this.

The structure of the day might be as follows:

1 Opening and introduction.
2 The two participating groups confer separately for one hour about the attitudes and the behaviour of the other group that they see as obstacles to their effectiveness. They also predict the opinions of the other group on this matter.
3 Joint meetings of around 45 minutes are held about the results of the subgroups. Participants may not enter into discussion; they may ask for clarification or examples until it is clear what is meant by each point and why it is felt to be an obstacle.
4 The groups talk separately about the results of the general discussion. They ask themselves how 'we' might be able to reduce the bottlenecks important to the other group. In a brainstorming session, a list of possibilities is drawn up.
5 In a general session, possibilities are exchanged and clarified; attempts are made to reach agreements.

TRAINING

A large number of training programmes are available at present to develop people's capacity for high-quality cooperation. These programmes concern:

- Discussion techniques
- Meeting skills, negotiating
- Problem solving, decision making
- Personal presentation
- Conflict management
- Personal effectiveness in groups
- Selling skills, customer contact, account management
- Management style
- Team development and group dynamics.

Since the 1950s the further development of knowledge and skills in these fields has been actively pursued. The abundance of material sometimes makes us lose sight of the fact that the development of social expertise ultimately depends on only a few skills: listening closely, empathy and the ability to provide and receive information regarding behavioural effects (feedback).

The development of our views in relation to these fields has by no means come to a halt. For a while the skills to handle contradictions, for example, were only weakly represented, if at all. This situation has been improved over the past five years. It is also curious to see that no consensus has been reached in the two fields we have been working in most intensively: leadership and problem solving. The field of leadership constantly produces controversies between the adherents of various grid systems, style quadrants and ever-different fundamental dimensions. Also remarkable is the fact that there is no empirical foundation worth mentioning for the problem-solving models which have been described extensively (namely various successive phases).

This remains a rather fashionable terrain, which continuously provides room for new trends and alternative approaches. Is the one-minute manager still popular? Is intuition once again the magic word? Are we ready to discard quality circles for quality problems?

The number of training activities aimed at the quality of cooperation is still increasing, and rightly so. It is interesting to see how the initial enthusiasm in terms of human development has been replaced by a down-to-earth and instrumental approach. It *pays* to develop these skills. They are needed if we want to be able to take on competitors and to prevent internal rumpus.

Elements of a training programme

The ability to function in teams can be stimulated through programmes of systematic communication improvement. We recommend that such a programme be combined with a plan aimed at improving results. Such a combination will clearly show that there is more to the process than merely interesting and positive skills. Even concepts such as improvement of culture, style of interaction and cooperation climate are too non-committal and too vague. We are referring to highly necessary and practical matters which are simply indispensable if we wish to improve results. Our experience has shown that projects in the fields of quality and customer orientation can get completely bogged down owing to cooperation problems. These problems provide the right occasion for introducing a training and educational programme.

The elements of such a programme are twofold. Improvement in communication is achieved by:

- Meeting skills and problem solving
- Constructive negotiating
- Coping with contradictions
- Personal effectiveness
- Team development.

Improved results are achieved by:

- Quality
- Customer orientation, external and internal
- Development of result indicators
- Work with those indicators
- Step-by-step plans to improve results.

Developments

It remains problematical to provide clear standards for the complexity of working relationships within and between organizations. Recommending openness, trust, directness and empathy as good qualities, and leaving it at that, is too simple. Working relationships are intrinsically ambivalent. They are characterized by cooperation *and* competition. People must also distinguish and present themselves, score, get ahead and do better than their competitors. In this context, solidity, tenacity and perseverance, even if not everybody agrees, are good qualities. These qualities are also enhanced by the tendency to structure organizations increasingly in relatively small units which must each show its own results. At the same time, one must be able (more so than in the past) to function in teams and to maintain a large network.

The tension balance between cooperation and competition always plays a part in relationships between people. Aspects of this balance are tensions surrounding the distribution of authority and dependence, the distribution of scarce goods, and the opportunities for expressing emotions, sympathy and a personal identity. The distribution of matters such as prestige, interesting and meaningful work, future career and training possibilities among people is not automatically without tension. There is always a more or less regulated tug-of-war. At the same time, it is often to everyone's advantage that mutual dependence, common outward power, consensus and shared identity are done justice and developed further.

People are increasingly expected to be capable of flexible cooperation *and* of showing results. This is not limited to interpersonal relationships. The same feature characterizes relationships between teams, between departments and between company units. We function increasingly in networks of negotiating relationships. To be able to do this, we need a social repertoire which unites ostensibly incompatible elements: flexibility *and* tenacity; informal relationships *and* self-assertion; the desire to work it out together *and* the need to hold on to personal interests. Differentiation of this repertoire is an ongoing process. Take for example the development towards both increased personal discipline and more room for spontaneous emotions, which has become more and more obvious in recent years. A second development concerns managing hierarchical differences in organizations. On the one hand, the hierarchy is not tampered with. The fact that there are disparities in the hierarchy does not pose any real problem. On the other hand, people have become more sensitive to expressions of superiority or subordination. Hierarchical differences as they were once shown in behaviour can no longer be expressed in this manner.

We are dealing with changing behavioural standards. These changes can be clarified by showing how past conduct related to superiority is experienced today, as in table 17.2 (Gomperts, 1987). The corollary is that conduct which is seen now as informal, easy, relaxed and creative is possibly viewed by old-style managers as coarse, impertinent, obtrusive and rash.

TABLE 17.2 Changing appreciation of expressions of superiority and subordination

Past	Present
Dedicated	Subservient
Modest	Socially anxious
Correct	Stiff
Respectable	Inhibited
Dignified	Conceited
Sturdy	Boastful
Distinguished	Arrogant
Decisive	Ambitious

There is no objection to hierarchical differences, but those involved should not express these disparities directly in their conduct. If they do, the effect will be irritation, cooling and formalization of the relationship. In this context, people show an increasing sensitivity to trifles such as loudness of voice, over-articulation, a fixed posture or facial expression, and claiming a disproportionate amount of speaking time.

A tendency towards more informal and relaxed conduct is visible. Those who have mastered this conduct gain status, especially if they are able to realize a certain amount of room for creativity and spontaneous feelings. The paradox here is that this increasingly loose and uninhibited conduct makes higher demands on the social skills than more standardized and patterned behaviour, which was once associated with the hierarchy. We could almost speak of compulsory informality. There is widespread concern for and insecurity about the presentation of self: 'Am I making the right impression?' This can result in behavioural obstructions, ranging from clamming up completely to acting overly equal and genial.

What we are talking about here are learning processes, which develop in front of our eyes and which involve everybody. These processes are roughly taking the direction of a more flexible regulation of emotions and the development of more differentiated conduct between tolerant and authoritarian, between distant and affective. This development is more than a recent fad. It is a long-standing and continuing change in the interdependencies between people and in the conduct and social standards people develop in their mutual dependence (Elias 1978, 1982).

Improved communication and attention to styles of cooperation are not fads either. They will occupy people in organizations to a considerably larger extent than is now the case. The critical success factor for each individual is keeping alert his own learning ability in the field of cooperation. This is not very hard, provided one remains open to signals from others regarding the effects of attitude and conduct.

CONCLUSIONS

The quality of cooperation is the crucial factor in motivating employees. It is also the most difficult factor to influence. One determining element is the behaviour of managers setting an example.

The behaviour referred to is not complex, but the development of it does depend on the desire and ability to learn. In other words, it is necessary to be curious about your own social effectiveness, and to encourage specific feedback and possible suggestions for improvement. This presumes an awareness of increasing dependence, both vertically between different echelons and horizontally between departments and disciplines. Sometimes this awareness is lacking. Formalized distance and clear boundaries can sometimes be very convenient.

If the awareness of mutual dependence is present, then a basis is provided for explicit and systematic improvement in the quality of cooperation. Managers and team members will have to take a few steps on this path together consciously. That learned in this way is more easily retained than the learning experiences gained in open groups. To provide safety and security, well-structured programmes and various aids have been developed. A few examples are presented in this chapter.

A complicating factor is the twofold nature of social skills: cooperation *and* competition; functioning well in teams *and* distinguishing oneself. A second complication is the gradual change in standards of conduct, for example regarding the appreciation of behaviour linked with hierarchical differences.

APPENDIX: SUPPORTING INSTRUMENTS

In this appendix we present several forms which can serve as aids in discussing the functioning of teams and persons. These instruments are used to evaluate and improve existing communication situations. They are sometimes used in training situations. The first two forms ('Result-oriented working' and 'Dominant communication style') are suitable for short evaluations at the end of a meeting. The forms 'Group standards' and 'Personal feedback behaviour' require more time.

If the notions of style of cooperation, quality of communication and corporate culture are still a bit vague, we recommend that you look at these forms. They specify the phenomena and behaviour which go with concepts such as corporate culture and style of interaction.

Participants generally sense whether this type of instrument suits them. If one feels that the instrument requires a great deal of effort and strain, we recommend bringing in a person who has some experience in this field. He can act as chairman and guide the discussion in the direction of improvement agreements.

RESULT-ORIENTED WORKING

Evaluation of the meeting in terms of:

(a) The results
(b) The utilization of mutual knowledge and experience.

Please circle the answers that best reflect your reaction to this meeting.

	Agree		Disagree	
	Strongly	Somewhat	Somewhat	Strongly
1 The result of this meeting was worth the time invested.	YES	yes	no	NO
2 I was given sufficient opportunity to explain my ideas about the subjects.	YES	yes	no	NO
3 This was an efficient meeting.	YES	yes	no	NO
4 The participants effectively utilized my knowledge regarding the subjects under discussion.	YES	yes	no	NO
5 The essential issues were not discussed.	YES	yes	no	NO
6 I had plenty of opportunity to influence the final conclusions and decisions.	YES	yes	no	NO

DOMINANT COMMUNICATION STYLE

Which of the following three styles dominated in this meeting?

Cooperation	Negotiation	Fighting
People try to understand one another and to see the other's point of view.	Understanding the other side is seen as a tactical instrument.	People don't want to understand the other side; aversion to empathy.
Commitment to one particular solution is deliberately delayed as long as possible.	Strong preference for a particular solution is shown, but margins and concessions are taken for granted.	Absolute preference for own solution is expressed at every opportunity.
Differences of opinion are seen as a joint problem.	Differences of opinion are seen as a clash between different but mutually dependent interests.	Difference of opinion is seen as a question of win or lose.
People present their own goals as accurately as possible.	People exaggerate their own interests, but are always on the look-out for common interests and overlaps.	Differences in objectives and superiority of own goals are emphasized.
Weak points and personal problems can be openly discussed.	Personal problems are hidden or presented circumspectly.	There is no such thing as personal problems.
Solutions are tested against their consequences. Principles provide common criteria.	Solutions are tested for feasibility. Principles are sometimes used as a lever, sometimes as a touchstone.	One's own solution is not only a question of being right, but also a matter of higher principles.
Personal irritations are expressed to clear the air of tensions that could hamper future cooperation.	Personal irritations are suppressed or ventilated indirectly (humour). Efforts are made to keep the atmosphere pleasant.	Irritations confirm existing negative images. No actions for improvement are taken.
Outside expertise is readily called in to aid the decision making.	Neutral outsiders are brought in only if there is complete deadlock.	Neutral outsiders are not welcome, only supporters.

GROUP STANDARDS FOR THE APPROACH TO PROBLEMS

Please indicate the degree in which the statements below characterize the meeting:

n = normal (occurs very often or regularly)
nn = not normal (happens occasionally or never).

		n	nn
1	Problems are discussed extensively, until everybody understands the issue.	☐	☐
2	The atmosphere is reasonably open and relaxed.	☐	☐
3	People come to the meeting not knowing what it will be about.	☐	☐
4	There is a tendency to provide solutions before the problem is thought through.	☐	☐
5	The pros and cons of alternative solutions are weighed carefully.	☐	☐
6	People's ideas are taken seriously.	☐	☐
7	One person sums up from time to time.	☐	☐
8	Decisions often remain vague – in terms of both what exactly has been decided and who is going to do what.	☐	☐
9	Many people say next to nothing.	☐	☐
10	On certain issues people refrain from committing themselves.	☐	☐
11	The meeting contains fractions and subgroups that thwart each other.	☐	☐
12	The meeting obviously has low priority: participants frequently cancel because something has come up.	☐	☐
13	People easily break agreements made during the meeting if this suits them better.	☐	☐
14	The results of the meeting are worth the time and effort.	☐	☐
15	Dissatisfaction with the way things go is expressed during the meeting.	☐	☐
16	People feel bound by the decisions made during the meeting.	☐	☐
17	The opinions of the participants frequently differ from the decision taken by the chairman.	☐	☐
18	The same issues keep coming back at every meeting.	☐	☐

PERSONAL FEEDBACK: STIMULATING BEHAVIOUR

1 Clear, concise formulation.
2 Continuing to ask questions when something is not clear.
3 Remaining concrete.
4 Giving your opinion freely.
5 Showing the outline.
6 Introducing humour at the appropriate times.
7 Trying to get backgrounds and preconceptions to the surface in the case of differing opinions.
8 Keeping an eye on the purpose of the meeting.
9 Putting others at ease.
10 Summarizing frequently.
11 Taking initiative.
12 Encouraging non-talkers to express themselves.
13 Monitoring progress.
14 Preparing thoroughly for the meeting.
15 Expressing interest in what others have to say.
16 Being open.
17 Trying to make tensions and conflict discussible.
18 Coordinating.
19 Activating and stimulating the group.
20 Getting to the heart of matters quickly.
21 Trying to combine ideas and proposals.
22 Not keeping your options open, stating your opinion clearly.
23 Winding up the discussion, verifying the decisions made.
24 Asking participants who are obviously irritated what is bothering them.
25 Being critical of the way the meeting is proceeding.
26 Elaborating on the ideas of group members.
27 Disagreeing with your superior if you believe your view on the issue is better.
28 Checking support, testing group opinion.
29 Telling others what you really think of their contribution.
30 Examining established procedures critically: 'Why do we do things this way?'
31 Making sure you know exactly what someone means before agreeing or disagreeing.
32 Creating clarity about what it is people are doing at a particular moment.
33 Picking up ideas presented by others, doing something with them, helping to develop them further.
34 Showing initiative and involvement.

PERSONAL FEEDBACK: IMPEDING BEHAVIOUR

1 Being afraid to show initiative.
2 Thinking in black and white.
3 Covering up problems to avoid tensions.
4 Rigidly holding on to something, coming back to the same thing again and again.
5 Defensive reaction, being quick to take offence, thin skinned.
6 Tendency to dominate, aggressive attitude, attacking others.
7 Not listening to the meaning behind other people's words.
8 Relating own prestige to statements made.
9 Underestimating yourself.
10 Being dependent, expressing helplessness, falling back on others.
11 Being critical while remaining uninvolved.
12 Unclear formulation.
13 Constantly judging others.
14 Giving insufficient space to others.
15 Not taking up the course of the discussion, digressing.
16 Being argumentative, clever.
17 Not noticing the needs of the group.
18 Lack of understanding of the effects of own behaviour on the group.
19 Using the group as a sounding board for own ideas.
20 Wanting to make an impression, seeking recognition, showing off.
21 Being the clown.
22 Talk first, think later.
23 Beating about the bush.
24 Asking few questions or none at all.
25 Asking questions, but in an interrogation style.
26 Losing sight of the purpose of the meeting.
27 Providing few practical examples or personal experiences, if any.
28 Ostentatious silence.
29 Focused on the chairman instead of the subject under discussion.
30 Being afraid to say what you really think about it.
31 Too abstract.
32 Giving too many concrete examples, so people can't see the wood for the trees.
33 Remaining non-committal, keeping things in a general perspective.

REFERENCES AND FURTHER READING

Elias, N. 1978: *The Civilizing Process*. New York: Pantheon.
Elias, N. 1982: *The Court Society*. Oxford: Basil Blackwell.
Fortune, 1987: Goodbye corporate staff. December, 116.
Gomperts, W. 1987: De opkomst van de sociale fobie. *Sociologisch Tijdschrift*, Jaargang 13, Nr. 4 Feb. 1987, 669–725.
Mastenbroek, W.F.G. 1987: *Conflict Management and Organization Development*. Chichester, New York: Wiley.
Mastenbroek, W.F.G. 1989: *Negotiate!* Oxford: Basil Blackwell.
Ouchie, W.G. 1981: *Theory Z*. Reading, Mass.: Addison-Wesley.
Peters, T.J. and Austin, N. 1985: *A Passion for Excellence*. New York: Random House.
Peters, T.J. and Waterman, R.H. 1982: *In Search of Excellence*. New York: Harper and Row.
Wrapp, H.E. 1984: Good managers don't make policy decisions. *Harvard Business Review*.

PART V
Step-by-step plans and programmes

18

Quality improvement by means of programme management

PIETERJAN VAN DELDEN

INTRODUCTION

Seldom has any organizational theme emancipated itself as rapidly as quality control. In a few years the care for perfect products and flexible services has evolved from a monitoring function to a management technique. This pursuit of quality has produced new approaches and methods for managers and consultants. The combination of Japanese examples, internationalization of markets and logistic innovations created a force which inspired brave change projects whose primary point of departure was quality improvement.

This impulse generates new challenges and opportunities for the practice of change. Quality improvement professes to be an approach which renders industrial processes controllable, so that they offer the opportunity to perfect products and services with simultaneous efficiency increases. However, the growing attention to this subject has not yet resulted in elaborate research into the effects of quality actions. It is obviously too early yet, or the goals have not been formulated clearly enough.

The first experiences on a project level, however, have been acquired by now. Sometimes the results are encouraging, leading to a shift from loss-making to profitable situations. In other cases results fail to materialize or they turn out to be temporary. The question is whether quality improvement as a change objective and management technique is strong enough to survive the current wave of fashionable interest.

What results can we reasonably expect, and which change problems will occur in this context?

ADVANTAGES OF THE QUALITY APPROACH

The rapid rise of quality improvement is related to the strategic upgrading of primary processes in organizations. Japanese companies showed that, by using quality techniques and sophisticated process control, better results could be obtained than by automation and logistic planning. This is one of the reasons the quality approach has been welcomed in the US and Europe as a new perspective for surviving as an organization in an increasingly chaotic environment (Peters, 1987).

Companies and ministries have awarded quality control a strategic position in their policy plans: on a European market, companies will be positioned on this basis in the future. Quality improvement and customer orientation are the direct and practical tools with which the customer groups must be approached and retained. Many products and services are routine, so the trick is to add a service edge.

This strategic employment of quality control is still a long way from being mastered. The most obvious approach is to tackle all organizational and management problems from this perspective. One can go at communication problems, for example, using the model of the internal customer–supplier relation. A weak market position can be counteracted by a new quality image. The label 'quality' can be attached to everything, and this feeds the temptation to start campaigns, fanning out in all directions, which are supposed to stimulate all employees to join in.

This trend appears to have passed its peak by now: the days of the hangar meetings are over. Old defects in the organization, personal limitations of board and middle management, and difficult suppliers can quickly trip up new concepts. At present, well-organized pilot projects, solid preparation and training are the leading concepts. Quality control is becoming a down-to-earth theme.

The quality theme now enjoys a wide popularity. In 1987, an estimated 2000 companies in The Netherlands were engaged in fundamental quality improvement (Project Group Quality Policy, 1987). In industry, 92 per cent of companies feel that quality control is part of the manager's duties and daily routine. However, complete quality control is not applied very often, probably only by 2 to 6 per cent of companies.

In the process of maturing, quality improvement as a change approach also incorporates elements from previous approaches. Many managers and consultants have experience in organizational development, strategic policy making and internal entrepreneurship, and they use their knowledge in the area of quality. Not all that glitters in conference folders is new. Yet there are differences. Three pluses of the quality approach force themselves upon us in particular:

- A quality approach offers the advantage of *concrete improvement goals*. The quality is measured in terms of product specifications or result indicators (Mastenbroek, 1990). Industry in particular has gained a lot of experience in this area, so that there is some certainty about the success chances of improvement goals. The appealing thing here is that it concerns tangible, formal improvements.

- Quality requires relatively *few investments* in terms of means or people. High demands are made on the reliability of equipment and the expertise of personnel, but no large and sometimes risky expenditures are necessary, which they sometimes are for product or market innovation. As a result, relatively limited investments in a quality programme can sometimes yield fairly high cost savings through fewer mistakes and breakdowns.

- Quality control is a *motivating and inspiring theme*. As a Philips manager once put it: you simply can't be against it. Quality improvement fits the personal needs of people to work professionally or to be of service to customers. Basically, it affects all employees. A quality action can stimulate the execution of self-control tasks which have been ignored for years.

Therefore quality improvement has the advantage of being a relatively simple (and cheap) approach which can yield considerable results. As a technique for change it may appeal to a wide group, especially in combination with the concept of internal customer–supplier relations. In this way it distinguishes itself in a positive sense from product or process innovations, which are generally prepared without the involvement of the operational specialists, and which for that reason can have a disruptive effect on the operational routine. Quality improvement usually takes the form of many small steps, which are easier to integrate in the operations (see figure 18.1: van Delden and van Ham, 1986).

A quality approach is practical and concrete, and it also provides clues for a broader approach to improving organizations. An added point is that the quality theme is very suitable for translation into an organizational mission. Quality and customer orientation have everything to do with organizational culture, and for that reason are often emphasized in internal corporate image campaigns. It should be noted that there is

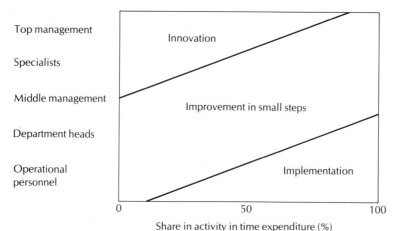

FIGURE 18.1 Contribution of activities per echelon

a risk here of losing the concrete and measurable aspects of quality, if campaigns are reduced to sloganeering.

PROGRAMME MANAGEMENT

It is often pointed out that quality improvement is a process which will take years to pay off. Very few organizations have taken this lesson to heart and actually developed quality control carefully and gradually. On the contrary, in recent years many attempts have been made in the form of a quality campaign to change organizational culture and operational methods rapidly. This can result in problems.

All-embracing attempts to introduce quality control quickly in an organization require a considerable effort from management. This change approach can be typified as a form of programme management. Vrakking (1986) describes this as 'managing various interrelated projects, which together result in a desired dominant development of an organization'. This type of change campaign is rather vulnerable. Vrakking lists several pitfalls in programme management. In the example in the next paragraph, loss of attention in the organization can occur as a result of too many change actions. Competition can emerge between the projects; there is a lack of exchange and learning between projects. An unclear or tense relationship with the existing organization can lead to the results of the change programme not being integrated in the work of departments, or the established culture and structure of management meetings are not suited to support the changes.

For example, in the context of a quality action the employees of a large administrative organization were invited to set up improvement groups, which were to provide solutions for practical problems and mistakes. One group tackled the problem of the many misunderstandings in the communication between financial specialists and the department of word processing. It turned out to be a tough job to go through all the procedures systematically. It took the improvement group almost a year to present well-founded proposals. Unfortunately, during this period attention to this problem had ebbed away, partly because the set-up of the word processing department had come into question. The work done by the improvement group 'would be of great use in further decision making' and subsequently did not get the attention it deserved.

If programme management is used too much as a convenient crowbar, there is a great risk that it won't fit existing routines and operational patterns and the accompanying attitudes and skills. The same applies to actions in the area of quality improvement. Vinkenburg (1988) examined quality projects in the service sector and found that several problems recur frequently. The set-up of projects if often improvised and is rarely based on knowledge of customer needs. Quality problems which transgress departmental boundaries are often very difficult to manage.

A strong appeal is made to some groups (middle management, operational employees), and this requires a large amount of loyalty and clarity regarding policy. This in turn requires a clear vision from top management, which should be presented with credibility and integrity. Vinkenburg remarks that structured action programmes are seldom used. This means that programme management can become the victim of its own lack of coherence, which can damage the desired results.

CRITICAL FACTORS

Quality improvement by programme management is popular but vulnerable. There is a strong temptation to track down a few obvious bottlenecks or improvement issues, to focus all energy on them and in this way to obtain quickly some tangible results. Early successes are needed to keep the process of change going. That is a basic truth, but the problem which emerges then – that old routines turn out to be stronger than the quality drive – is more difficult and therefore a less attractive action object. In other words, there is a dilemma between short term and long term.

The trick is to develop a change programme which not only yields quick results, but also gradually produces improvements in existing routines and organizational structure. Such a change programme will have to meet four critical conditions. These will be described below with the aid of practical examples.

Quality assessment

The power of the quality approach is located in the concrete standards by which products and services are assessed. This implies that initially vague ideas and opinions about 'our quality' are transformed into criteria. Several possibilities present themselves. A customer perception evaluation can provide an image of the appreciation of the product compared with the products of others. At the same time management can make a list of indicators, to be used internally as an audit. The best solution for testing performance against the desired quality profile is often a mix of external research and internal evaluation.

In general assessment is required of the following quality dimensions:

- Completeness of the product and service package
- Personal professionalism and know-how
- Organizational flexibility, customized delivery
- Logistic planning, punctuality
- Attention to the individual customer, rendering of service
- Clarity of presentation, image
- Internal efficiency, cost control.

The importance of a specific, personal company form of quality assessment is considerable. It directs new products and projects. Using quality indicators, the existing organization can hold ingrained routines and procedures up to the light. Evaluating customer satisfaction can uncover organizational weaknesses such as crippled communication between departments, and clumsy ordering or delivery procedures. In many cases this kind of evaluation points out the introvert functioning of units which have little contact with customers. In particular, professional organizations soon tend to derive their self-image from their own expert knowledge or discipline instead of basing it on the assessments made by customers and clients.

For example, a group of instructors in an educational organization took the initiative for brainstorming sessions about quality improvement.

This was regarded as a plus activity: the institute was already functioning well, and the only question was whether improvements might be possible here and there. Both instructors and students were asked to write down a list of strong and weak points in the institute.

The instructors judged the quality of the education to be good in general, but had some doubts about internal communication. The students gave no opinion on this; they experienced the general atmosphere as pleasant, but had a great deal of criticism concerning the lack of integration in the curriculum. It was established that both groups used widely differing standards to judge the educational quality. Instructors thought their personal skills were very important, with an emphasis on specialist understanding. Students were more interested in their presentation styles and the coherence between subjects. These differences made it difficult to achieve an improvement programme which could be supported by all.

Quality awareness

Driving back faults in production or anticipating customer wishes requires dedication from the employees. Not only must they be loyal to the quality action, they should also regard it as a personal challenge. Many quality campaigns are aimed at quickly and deeply convincing a wide group in the organization. Plenary meetings, information actions, changes in house style, quality trophies and questionnaires are often used to this end. In addition we see voluntary quality groups, feedback of customer assessments, training and workshops.

The problem frequently is that the employees are asked to make an extra effort, but they generally get very little in return. Research has shown that quality projects hardly affect the quality of the work (van Delden and Jansen, 1987). Quality improvement is often supported by more explicit performance standards and automation, which limit freedom of action, especially in regard to relatively unskilled labour. Professionals, on the other hand, frequently succeed in broadening the scope of their work through quality projects. In this way, quality actions can enlarge the existing differences between employees. This means that quality projects will be judged differently by different groups in the organization, depending on the way these projects will have a limiting or broadening effect on their work.

A desk clerk in a post office had the following remarks to make:

> I can only be friendly to customers if I know I have proper backing. If a customer wants a brochure and it takes me ten minutes to find it because things are not organized, then he will be fuming and I am the one he will

rage at. As chairman of the works council I put this to management time and time again: 'These things may not be important to you, but they are important for us. This is the only way to motivate your personnel.' We don't get the opportunity to prove it. What management actually does is say 'Desk clerks, be friendly' but they don't listen to what we have to say. (Drayer, 1988)

Quality awareness is a critical factor, because the initial enthusiasm of employees can die out for several reasons:

- The quality of the work can diminish.
- Employees feel their jobs are in danger.
- Managers have little time for details which are essential to the employees.
- Quality improvement is introduced not as a challenge to individual skills, but primarily as a sharpened performance standard.

Product improvement and quality awareness can reinforce each other if an organization stimulates for quality initiatives at the operational level. Operational processes and consultative structures can be designed towards this end, often more easily than those involved think. It requires primarily that information and training programmes are effectively geared for small improvement projects on the shop floor.

In a truck factory, for example, small conference rooms have been constructed which are adjacent to the shop floor. Experience showed that employees felt the need to conduct quality meetings as close as possible to the production process, because they felt at ease there. The company decided in favour of this investment to encourage the need of mechanics and inspectors to solve bottlenecks in production. This phenomenon really got off the ground after management had reacted quickly in earlier projects to proposed changes and improvements. The procedure of 'note a problem; set up a working group; present the results to management' has taken hold now, partly due to the fact that the mechanics can start on the improvements directly. In addition the company has guaranteed the nobody will lose his job as a result of quality proposals.

Quality management

Quality literature indicates in various ways that process control is a crucial condition for gradual improvement. Manufacturing processes must be able to guarantee zero defects, which is only possible in the long run if the causes of breakdowns and defects in the process are understood. To enable a shift from incidental successes to structural progress, it is necessary to control divergences, logistics, administrative procedures and continuation of the project. This requires an analysis of sources of interference and a focus on weak spots in systems and procedures. And that is why the rule of thumb is that management is responsible for 85 per cent of the quality failures and employees are responsible for only 15 per cent.

The individual employee is seldom in a position to tackle defective procedures and regulations. Managers have the duty and the skill to determine weaknesses in the organization and to get rid of them. Eliminating an untidy process defect or streamlining the administrative organization can be more effective than years of improvising and troubleshooting.

For example, the top management in a ministry embarked on a quality action enthusiastically. Officials were told to answer letters within a week, answer telephones before the third ring and not let a colleague's phone go on ringing. Notes and letters must be concise and more or less memo-like, and internal loyalty was to be increased by means of more information (partly by a more professional in-house magazine). After some time, the employees of the ministry reacted sceptically. Their criticism was that most of the delays were caused by time-consuming consultation procedures between the departments in the ministry, which had sometimes been at odds with each other for years. The lack of organizational coherence, however, had not been considered in the quality policy, because the top management was of the opinion that the primary goal should be the promotion of a result and a customer-oriented attitude in thought and action.

Structural quality improvement is often only possible if the tensions and problems in the primary processes of an organization are tackled. If this is not done, then there is a very real risk that the improvement pace will slow down after the initial successes. Small attempts at improvement in operations can be hampered by system defects: time-consuming procedures, inadequate automation, lack of budgetary freedom, over-informal agreements concerning service to customers, or a formalistic approach to customer complaints.

The trick is to translate, through the quality change programme, the formulated product specifications into system specifications. Important aspects of systems are:

- Procedures and responsibilities
- Administrative organization
- Flexibility of equipment

- Agreements with suppliers
- Freedom to act for employees.

All system factors (routines, equipment and other fixed elements in the operational process) must fit the quality requirements. Such an approach can be described as integral quality control: all the relevant processes and systems are assessed against the quality programme and adjusted. Blauw (1988) establishes that in fact this seldom happens. The control of primary functions is receiving more attention, but often in the sense of formalizing procedures. The mutual tuning of primary functions is often neglected.

A coherent implementation of changes in the various functions obviously requires a considerable management effort. If it works, the results can be spectacular. For example, owing to decreasing sales, the board of a restaurant chain was confronted with the necessity for quality improvement. In the past, improvement had primarily been pursued by the simultaneous decentralization and professionalization of management. It had become clear that this approach resulted in confusion about responsibilities. The new approach was characterized by:

- Development of central, specific quality standards based on experiments and customer research
- Investment in equipment in order to serve fresh dishes to large groups with more flexibility
- Development of a specific restaurant concept with a combination of service and self-service
- Improved terms of employment and intensive training of personnel.

This combination of measures created the possibility of sophisticated process control, in which increased attention to the customer went hand in hand with a rationalization of processes. Employees reacted enthusiastically, because they were given the means to supply the service expected of them. In the short term, it even resulted in attracting new groups of customers.

Quality policy

Quality improvement is a relatively new perspective for management. Historically it originates in quality control, an activity initially reserved for technicians in production. One result of this shop floor tradition of quality control is that it is often still seen as an operational problem or a tactical issue. Quality is seldom regarded strategically, in spite of sometimes massive company campaigns. The result is that quality as an objective is easily abandoned when other problems or actions demand attention. This can damage the theme's credibility.

In a meat packing company, for example, the employees were given the task of judging the quality of the product and rejecting batches if necessary. The packers could 'do quality' in turns. However, the company experienced considerable problems with peaks and lows in production. This was caused partly by the fact that the company wished to be very flexible towards customers and so had to deliver quickly. A result of this was that the quality standards were sometimes lowered a little during peak periods to prevent delays by rejection. That is why, after some time, there was little point in spending so much time on quality inspection in operations. 'Doing quality' became less frequent and also less popular among the employees.

A strategic choice for quality improvement implies that a sustained effort is made to link up this theme with other strategic decisions. If not, the chances are that the quality action will be pushed aside by a problem or a change which has risen on the priority ladder. A merger can unsettle all carefully elaborated quality measurements because the new partners have different standards. Cutbacks or reorganizations are at odds with the perspective of gradual improvements implicit in the quality notion.

For example, a municipal police force faced the task of making up for an automation lag. They had a choice between using a system which was already in place with other forces or developing their own system. Using the existing system, several useful applications would be available immediately, but adaptation to personal wishes was hardly possible. Developing a new system would provide more opportunities for customization, but this would require a much larger effort. The top management decided in favour of new development, because they wanted to give priority to support of operations. The main issues were reducing administrative work for the policemen on patrol, and improving coordination of the service to civilians and companies. The key notion was that the force as a whole must meet customers in a flexible manner. The eventual system consisted of a relational database, which the user could enter through different topics (address, registration number, nature of the violation/offence, person). The system was so user friendly that it became possible to fill out forms directly on screen. The time saved benefited police presence on the street.

Product innovations can be introduced suddenly by a group of developers in the company, quite apart from customer wishes or quality procedures, which only concerned the traditional products. This possible thwarting of quality actions shows that quality policy must always be tied in with other major policy operations. If not, quality policy will in the long run be limited to a few protected areas in the organization, where it will play a relatively minor role. This requires strategic determination.

IMPROVEMENT PERSPECTIVES

Assessment, awareness, management and policy have been described as critical factors which determine the viability of a quality project. The point is to go beyond the barrier between a short-term action and the improvement of organizational systems and routines. If this threshold is crossed, the successes of a quality approach will look different as well. Initially it is usually a matter of improvements resulting from simple system defects, which are easily changed: misunderstandings between departments, slipshod communication, badly designed order forms or defective instructions to personnel. Improving these things usually generates quick results and is inspiring.

It is more difficult to tackle structural system defects: automation that has been handled badly, lack of logistic planning, an excessive number of hierarchical levels in the organization or an unclear division of tasks between groups or departments. Improvements in these areas are longer in the making, but they are also more enduring. In other words, they are more capable of absorbing changes and disruptions, for example in product innovation or in serving a new group of customers.

Practice has shown that the results of quality projects can be located on widely differing levels. After the initial small successes, the following effects may occur:

- Improvement of products and services, often gradually in a long series of small changes

- Improved relations with customers, because their complaints and suggestions are taken seriously and are acted upon

- Reduced waste of effort and materials, because of improved assessment and application of expenditure or means

- Cost reduction as a result of increased budget control and a better understanding of the cost effectiveness of activities

- Stimulation of creativity by tapping new ideas and energy from a large group of employees

- Improved communication, because disturbances and defects which have been irritating everybody (for a long time) can now be discussed

- Increased job satisfaction for employees when they feel they have more grip on their own product.

So a quality programme may also result in many internal and subjective effects, which are however the necessary basis for better results in the market. It is remarkable that many companies and government organizations, after heavily publicized quality campaigns, have now shifted to more internally oriented improvement projects. Obviously, management have reached the conclusion that external product quality must be rooted firmly in the internal quality of the organization. If they were campaign leaders or product champions before, they now set themselves up as change masters. The external success must be carried by the internal inspiration.

REFERENCES

Blauw, J.N. 1988: *Towards Quality: integral quality control as innovation* (in Dutch). University of Twente.

Drayer, E. 1988: New slogans in an old company (in Dutch). *Vrij Nederland*, 24 December.

Mastenbroek, W.F.G. 1990: Information management, organizational design and organizational theory. *European Management Journal*, 8(1), 130–6.

Peters, T. 1987: *Thriving on Chaos*. New York: Knopf.

Project Group Quality Policy, Ministry of Economic Affairs, 1987: *The Netherlands: high time for quality* (in Dutch). NEHEM.

van Delden, P.J. and van Ham, C. 1986: The implementation of a quality drive in a multinational company. In A.J. Cozijnsen and W.J. Vrakking (eds), *Handboek Strategisch Innoveren* (in Dutch), Kluwer Nive.

van Delden, P.J. and Jansen, T. 1987: *Quality Control and the Quality of Labour* (in Dutch). NEHEM.

Vinkenburg, H. 1988: *Service and Profit: how 13 companies improve their service* (in Dutch). Deventer.

Vrakking, W.J. 1986: Organizational campaigning (in Dutch). Holland Consulting Group O & I 18.

19

Improving quality in the service business: dos and don'ts in working with quality programmes

WILLEM F.G. MASTENBROEK

INTRODUCTION

A few years ago a commercial bank set out on a large-scale project of quality improvement. The campaign was launched by a few top managers with much fanfare; spectacular events, special start-up days, posters and special quality symbols typified the first phase. Task forces and project groups set to work throughout the company and an extensive training programme was implemented. The central project organization, which coordinated all the efforts, had worked out a well-constructed 18-step plan that was to be used as a scenario.

Today the project is stagnating. Employees are disappointed. For the most part, the measurement and analysis techniques to which the expensive training programme devoted so much attention are not being applied. The top managers who launched the project now give the impression that they have lost both their interest and their enthusiasm; a few of them are even suggesting that 'now things are back to normal'. Many of the middle managers are being downright obstreperous; they feel that the blame is being thrust upon their shoulders, even though they never had any influence on the project. They were the ones who had to keep things moving despite the loss of their personnel to training and project group activities.

It is becoming increasingly apparent that, although there are plenty of ideas for improving quality, the old points of contention such as struggles for competencies, centralization versus decentralization and faulty communication and inflexible relations are making progress difficult. In a recent evaluation the central project group revealed that the project, with its carefully worked out 18-step plan and exemplary organization, had in fact stimulated bureaucratic tendencies, whereas the objective had been to convert rigidity and bureaucratization into motivation and entrepreneurial action. They are now looking for a way of breaking through the impasse.

What can we learn from this? Should we attempt to formulate quality programmes in even greater detail? Quite the opposite is true. I would like to present my views in the form of a simple three-step plan (figure 19.1). I also describe three conditions for success. These success conditions relate to all three steps, but each has a special relevance for a particular step (see figure 19.1). In addition, I discuss the ways that training and consultation can lend support.

The characteristics of the approach described here are as follows:

Simplicity of set-up   Although a three-step plan may look less impressive than an 18-step plan, there is very little danger that it will foster bureaucracy. It does not arouse exaggerated expectations, and it makes us face up to the reality of learning by doing.

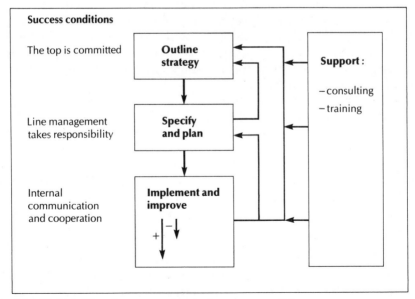

FIGURE 19.1 The three-step plan and success conditions

Role of top management   Outline a clear strategy and maintain progress. It is crucial that the organization's top management presents an unambiguous outline of strategy. This outline may be very concise; it might be formulated in two paragraphs. At the same time, top management must be tenacious in achieving step-by-step improvements. In this respect, a large-scale initial campaign is much less effective in the long run than continual stimulation to formulate plans and to progress within the established outline.

Those directly involved detail strategy   The strategy outline is not detailed by the organization's top management; it is elaborated on and specified by the next echelons. There is no heavy project organization; the line is responsible. Those involved do not necessarily have to keep all the same pace; as long as they continue to take part, individual units may move at their own speed.

OUTLINE STRATEGY

Top management decides to strengthen quality and to encourage a customer-oriented attitude both internally and externally. It presents this decision in a brief document; it is sometimes appended to the strategic plan, which indicates in what direction the key activities are to be developed in the coming years. More and more frequently we find a vision of the organization, its identity and management style forged together with a concise strategic plan into a sort of mission. This document serves as a basis for discussion and amendment by the next echelons of the organization.

In its simplest form, this document is no more than a policy outline, one in which the importance of better quality is explained and motivated, perhaps supplemented by a short slogan pointing out a few quality characteristics that are specific to the company, such as punctual, friendly, innovative, responsible and concerned. Such characteristics of quality are the central values within the policy outline. Using a different jargon, we might term them *critical success factors*. They are sometimes formulated on the basis of a study of what distinguishes the company from its competitors.

It is best to review the policy outline and to allow it to take shape in the next one or two management echelons. In this context, defining strategy is not merely the top management's affair; it extends deeper into the organization. This is an important point.

The draft of the strategy outline is thus presented to the next echelon, which may be asked for general reactions, additions or suggestions, and questions. The object of such a meeting is to inform managers and get them actively involved; this can only succeed if there is room for criticism, suggestions, and dialogue.

The next echelon in a publishing company remarked that it felt the policy outline was extremely open ended; practically every company nowadays claims it is working on quality and a customer orientation. Rather than launching into an explanation that it was not meant that way, the top manager kept the discussion focused on how the outline could be made more tangible. The top management and the next echelon reached a solution: to add a third point to quality and customer orientation, namely 'making results visible'.

In another situation, the next echelon brought up a long list of complaints and points of contention that dealt primarily with the standard operating procedures of several central departments. Management held an extra meeting to inventory these problems more systematically. Task forces were set up for the two most persistent and urgent problems; only then was attention turned to the policy outline.

This step of 'outline strategy' ends with a finalization of the outline and with agreements about its further elaboration, for which the next echelons bear the responsibility. A date is fixed on which to meet and exchange these plans. Sometimes the management groups involved plan interim horizontal exchanges to keep informed and to learn from one another's ideas.

Top management provides the impetus; this means there is no cumbersome project organization, but at most only a small group of consultants and trainers who possess the necessary knowledge and experience. They can serve as a sounding board, and they must make sure that supportive training is available.

SPECIFY AND PLAN

We cannot emphasize strongly enough that the company's line managers should take responsibility for the further elaboration of the general outline. In concrete terms, this means that line managers develop plans of action for ways in which they intend to improve quality and strengthen a customer orientation in their own organizational units. The same process is repeated at each level in the organization; each level states in concrete terms what quality and a customer orientation mean to it. This generally implies attention to three tracks:

Making quality and customer orientation visible   In other words, to measure is to know! What clocks show how well or how poorly we are doing? Examples of performance indicators in the retail trade are lines at cash desks, complaints, turnover per department or article group and per square metre, sales costs per square metre. Examples for a distribution centre are delivery time, delivery reliability and complaints. Sometimes assessment forms are used on which internal service customers score such aspects as quality of service and commitment and involvement.

Removing obstacles to quality and customer orientation A number of urgent problems often lie below the surface; in such cases discussion of quality and customer orientation brings them to the fore. Task forces are then set up to find solutions to the most urgent bottlenecks and obstacles.

The quality of the communication Meeting skills and communication and management style are sometimes unable to support the processes listed above. In such cases, a training programme aimed at improving communication can be useful.

A support group with the necessary expertise can do important work during this phase. Such a group can help managers to handle the discussions in their team; it can structure the three tracks and make concrete suggestions for progress. A support group can also arrange the horizontal exchanges among the managers of the various units. After all, these managers have all committed themselves to the formulation of a plan; it is highly motivating for them to know how their colleagues are getting on with it and to learn from one another.

This process of specifying and planning is repeated at each level of the company. Managers at each level formulate plans for ways in which quality and customer orientation can be introduced more deeply in their organizational units. Their plans are based in part on the ideas and possibilities of the next echelon on this topic. They also have a certain autonomy in accordance with the overall plan, in determining with the employees involved the indicators of quality and customer orientation for their own level. This can be expressed schematically as in figure 19.2.

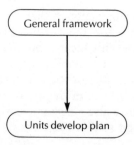

FIGURE 19.2 A two-step plan

The track of improving communication may be so important that it is decided to handle it separately from the very beginning. Sometimes skills and techniques, statistical and otherwise, for problem analysis and solution receive the most attention; in other cases, the emphasis may be placed on courses in client contacts. The yield of such training courses is greatly increased if they are integrated into an overall plan that the employees involved know and accept (figure 19.3).

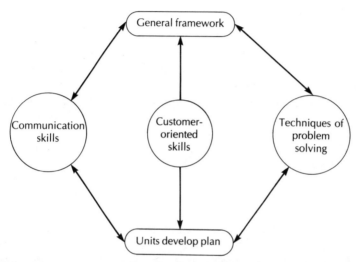

FIGURE 19.3 A two-step plan linked to training

To summarize, the phase of 'specify and plan' means that the employees involved must specify a limited number of critical quality areas – critical in the perception of (internal) clients. Next they must make agreements about how they will improve their performance in these areas, and when and how they will start measuring their performance. Some internal problems that deserve separate attention often arise at this point; in addition the quality of communication may need special attention.

IMPLEMENTATION AND IMPROVEMENT

The implementation phase focuses on the three tracks described above:

• Making visible quality and customer orientation

- Solving urgent problems
- Improving communication.

Organizations generally progress step by step on these tracks. 'Implementation' is an inadequate description of this phase: we are really talking about a process of continual improvement, one that takes on different emphases in the course of time.

To increase the chances of success, those involved should consider the following important matters:

1 To measure is to know, but measuring for whom? Making results visible can surely be an incentive for improving them, but an incentive is less likely to succeed if people believe that performance measurement is used primarily as a means of control for higher echelons. Management's steering should focus on the process of *making results visible* and improving them, not on controlling outcomes and calling people to account for them. This statement means that everyone, including those who are directly involved, must abide by a few rules. The most important of these are: scores serve as a platform for improving results; scores in themselves are unimportant, what counts is the trend; and rather than pass the buck, the involved parties must ask 'What can we do better?'

2 Certain central values, such as dynamism, punctuality or friendliness, are set down in the general framework. These values cannot be introduced on a whim; there are several ways to develop and strengthen them. One way is for company units to operationalize them in the form of *indicators*. This is no easy matter; in our experience it has taken place only on a limited scale. Nevertheless it is the best way to elevate dynamism, punctuality and friendliness above the level of catchwords with no obligations. Another way is to embed the central values in the appraisal system; still another is to hold evaluative talks with all employees at certain intervals about the extent to which they put these values into daily practice.

3 A customer orientation is one of the goals; this means an *internal customer orientation* as well as an external one. It is difficult for some people to understand that they should see the next in line as customers; because of their own expertise, some people think they themselves are qualified to judge. 'The customer does not really know what he is talking about', they say, 'Sometimes he can't even say exactly what he wants.' In view of their own expertise, or perhaps because of professional norms, people think they know better than the client does: such an attitude easily comes across as presumptuous and domineering. Because this attitude causes exter-

nal customers to leave, people are careful about adopting it with them; however, internal customers very often have no choice, and thus the way is paved for arrogant meddling. People still have to learn on occasion that professionalism and expertise must also be shown in understanding the customer and in willingness to think along with him or her in formulating attainable, realistic demands. These traits can be strengthened by having internal customers assess the amount of involvement, empathy and willingness to think along with them and to provide service.

4 Now and then *things will stagnate* and impasses will occur. Management's attention will sometimes waver. These things happen; people cannot be forced into obedience. It is inevitable that everyone will not move at the same pace, and we must not make an issue out of it. To each his own pace, now accelerating, now running ahead, often watching and waiting: these are facts of life. The philosophy behind this plan, that people bear the responsibility for carrying out their tasks, also extends to this field. This will cause a certain amount of tension; when units are extremely slow at starting or when they take no initiative at all, they are especially in danger of falling by the wayside. This must be resolved by discussing with the responsible managers how they plan to prevent such problems from occurring.

5 In time, results turn out to be increasingly dependent on the *quality of communication*. This means that there is a tendency towards an informal communication style with attention to acceptance and trust, as well as to more technical skills such as problem solving, meeting and negotiating, quality measurement techniques, and the analysis of causes and solutions. These skills do not come naturally; they must be encouraged and developed. Training programmes and resources for this purpose have been under development since the 1950s. More high-quality and relatively short modules are becoming available in these fields. The degree to which management is open to this factor is critical; setting behavioural examples, investing in the quality of vertical and horizontal communication, and evaluating the quality of their own meetings are matters in which they will have to take the first step.

Although these points may seem somewhat laborious, in reality they are not. Flexibility, a focus on immediate results, humour, trial and error: all these elements are part of the game. We are carried along with it by the competition and by societal developments. Even if we sit back and watch, we will still be drawn along, but we run a greater risk of making unnecessary mistakes and failing to keep up with our competitors.

To improve the chances of immediate attainments, here are a few tips:

- Encourage ideas with quick responses from higher echelons.
- Bring people into contact with clients.
- Reward quality and a customer orientation, for instance with a monthly award, a certificate or a cash bonus.
- In letters to the client use fewer 'wes' and more 'yous'.
- Provide the best parking spaces for the customers.
- Periodically consult a client panel.
- Formulate one point in which you are prominent or in the process of becoming so.
- Register complaints.
- Show that complaints are handled immediately.
- Make sure you can be reached by phone.

WORKING ON QUALITY

What this approach comes down to is the process of continually improving quality and working on a customer orientation both internally and externally. It is a method of management aimed at strengthening the company's or unit's competitive position by constantly working to improve results; each step in that direction, no matter how small, is welcome. It is not necessary to stimulate this approach with great fanfare; in fact, that may well be inadvisable. It is not a campaign; rather it is a manner of working. Little by little, it is strengthened and reinforced until it becomes a natural, permanent process.

A few things are fairly predictable at the start of such a process. It begins with a general framework in which quality and customer orientation are linked to the visible improvement of results; to measure is to know! As this track takes shape, a second track soon appears: the removal of concrete obstacles and irritations. This second track is sometimes expressed as a criticism of the organization and its management. The criticism can be dealt by tackling the most urgent bottlenecks. This second track may temporarily take precedence over the first. Management must first get some problems out of the way. Gradually a third track, that of the quality of communication, may appear. Then we must examine those activities that will improve horizontal and vertical communication, such as team development, occasionally across unit borders. This process of step-by-step improvement is stimulated by the regular feedback of performance indicators, which is in fact the driving force behind the entire process.

We can express this schematically as in figure 19.4. From the very beginning, there will be links to more fundamental matters in the fields of strategy, structure and culture. In the long run, particular adjustments sometimes crystallize in these areas. For example, adaptations are made to the organizational structure, so that units have a clearer responsibility about products and clients or the core business is formulated in a more down-to-earth manner. This is shown in the bottom track of the diagram.

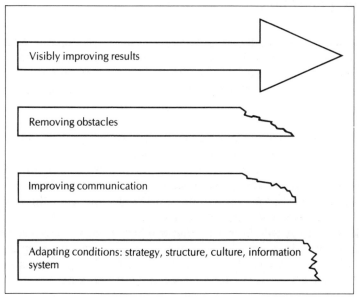

FIGURE 19.4 Working on quality: a multitrack approach.

To summarize a few important points:

- Large-scale manifestations are not worth the trouble; continual internal and external marketing are more effective.

- Not all units proceed at the same pace. Do not force them into line. Do, however, encourage horizontal exchange.

- There should be no separate project organization; the line is responsible. At most, only a small supporting team should be used.

- Quality improvement and a client orientation are interwoven with improving results. This is particularly true in commercial services.

- Facilitating the process is something entirely different from controlling results and calling people to account.

- Work on improving communication at the same time.

- What we are in fact trying to do is to ingrain an attitude of working on continual improvement as a natural habit in all echelons and units of the organization.

CONCLUSIONS

Every step-by-step plan has a deceptive aspect: it suggests logic and systematics that cannot be found in practice. There often seems to be very little system and yet very sensible things take place: a management team orients itself; sometimes plans take a fixed shape; people start work on a project and management waits to see what will come of it. If, at this point, they observe that the organization is not yet ready for it, they may come up with the idea of a campaign; when this does not achieve the desired result, they may start a training programme. Learning by doing is fine, but it can lead to needless bickering and unnecessary efforts; this is where the experiences of others can be helpful.

This chapter is an attempt to distil a few lessons from those experiences. It presents a vision, a thread to be followed, and thus offers a handle. Questions will often arise that will have to be answered according to the specific situation. For example, what if a unit manager is in no mood to go step by step, but simply wants to start? A possible approach is summarized here in the form of a ten-point checklist:

1 Pay more attention to the ideas and suggestions of our employees and our clients, both internal and external.
2 Become acquainted with the experiences of others.
3 Inventory the obstacles to effectiveness and remove them.
4 Improve complaint handling and show it.
5 Improve team communication.
6 Increase the accessibility of clients (internal and external). How often does the telephone ring?
7 Break down the pigeon-hole mentality; work more integrally; build bridges, not partitions.
8 Get the opinions of your (internal) clients.

9 Measure your results on a few items, for instance costs and products, yields, one or two service aspects; record them, keep track of the trends.

10 Make an improvement plan for your own unit by discussing the following points:

(a) Who are our clients?

(b) How do we perform in the eyes of our clients?

(c) On what critical factors can we perform better?

(d) How will we work on this?

Every manager who wants to do something about quality and customer orientation can go through these ten points with his employees, picking out those that are feasible in their particular situation. If they feel that these ten points are not enough to go on, or if they choose the point 'Become acquainted with the experiences of others', this book can offer more information.

20

Epilogue: managing for quality in the service sector

WILLEM F.G. MASTENBROEK, GERCO C. EZERMAN and LEO A.F.M. KERKLAAN

INTRODUCTION

In 1983 the Holland Consulting Group obtained its first assignments in the area of quality improvement in the service sector. A few years later the first articles were taking shape. This process of reflection on experiences continues to the present day, and finds its expression in this volume.

The chapters can be read separately. However, they are also complementary. Where one emphasizes the methodological aspects of quality improvement, a second focuses on the necessity to work also on the quality of cooperation. A third chapter stipulates that quality improvement is most easily realized in organizations which consist of result-responsible units, and a fourth describes the implementation of quality improvement. Part V, 'Step-by-step plans and programmes', contains chapters which integrate our views.

It will have become obvious from the contributions that we think in terms of various complementary and mutually reinforcing forces. Growing towards business units, improving cooperation, working with quality methods, having a simple implementation strategy via the line organization: all of these factors together determine the success of a quality improvement process. The interrelation between these factors has been described in the previous two chapters.

This epilogue contains a review of some important elements of quality improvement. A few issues will be accentuated. In conclusion a brief résumé of this book will be presented.

STIMULATING CONDITIONS

The first element is that a quality programme has better chances of success if the design of an organization includes a good balance on the tension axis central–decentral. If the organization consists on the one hand of result-responsible units, and on the other of a central management focused on development of a mission, on support and on learning from one another, then the specification and visibility of unit results and quality achievements are facilitated. This type of organizational design enables everybody to feel responsible for the quality of the service from his/her own field of responsibility.

We observe the tendency to form organizations in this way all around us. In our opinion this does not necessarily mean that organizations which do not (as yet) have such a structure cannot start on systematic quality improvement. In fact, every unit within every company can initiate quality improvement; however, if one lacks the incentive of responsibility for results, then it will be more difficult to appeal to the quality motivation in that particular unit.

QUALITY POLICY: THE MISSION

We do see the availability of a quality mission as an important condition. This policy should be based on the following key questions:

- Which (internal or external) customers do we have?

- Which services and products do we supply?

- What are the most important service items for the customers?

- What is the competition up to?

- What are we going to improve by what actions?

Several chapters emphasize that the development of quality policy is not merely a top–down matter; active involvement of middle management is indispensable. We select these key questions because they are important on all levels and to all units. Clear formulation of a quality mission is in fact the first step in a quality improvement process.

ORGANIZING QUALITY IMPROVEMENT

Next is the question: how do we organize the process of quality improvement? The answer provided by several chapters in this book is pithy: in the line. Quality improvement is realized in the normal work and communication processes:

- Existing communication structures

- Existing personnel policy: training, recruitment and selection

- Existing contracting processes: management contracts, unit action plans and evaluation meetings.

Do not rig up a project organization which thinks about quality while the rest of the organization is waiting for it!

Nevertheless, a separate service group will be necessary, especially in the area of support. It will address matters such as:

- Gathering and distributing the results of quality actions

- Providing support to the organizational units by means of consulting and training

- Coordinating quality actions to prevent all departments approaching customers with customer research simultaneously and separately.

Our experience has shown that creating a small service group for these supporting tasks is very effective. This group could consist of one or two line managers and some internal or external trainers and consultants. Occasionally a group like this is useful to tackle a specific quality problem which concerns several units.

That brings up the problem of integrated innovation. One of our clients, a large municipal transportation company, has several adjoining change processes:

- Marketing efforts
- Quality programmes
- Logistic projects
- Restructuring the organization
- Computerization.

These innovation processes must be geared for one another, and this tuning is the responsibility of top and higher management. Chapter 2 describes how innovations in the areas of structure, culture, strategy and information systems can be integrated in a consistent and mutually supportive design.

METHODS FOR QUALITY IMPROVEMENT

The fourth element consists of the application of a number of methods:

- Systematic inventory of quality problems
- Organizing customer involvement
- Formulating indicators
- Using measuring instruments.

The art is to keep this simple. This means setting priorities and selecting only a few critical performance areas with corresponding indicators.

In more production-oriented units of service organizations (administration, mail distribution, house printer), an arsenal of techniques from the world of quality circles is also available. These methods are more refined forms of attaining the correct problem diagnoses and choice of solutions; examples include Pareto analysis and Ishikawa diagrams. We have not addressed these methods in this book at length. Extensive publications on the subject are widely available. In service organizations it often suffices if feedback from customers is more structured, if indicators are developed and if the results per indicator are examined and improved by responsible line managers and their teams.

It is important that the entire department is involved in the application of these methods. In the case of interdepartmental problems the same methods can be applied by interdepartmental teams, focusing on interface problems such as internal customer orientation combined with visible results.

IMPLEMENTATION STRATEGIES

The whole set of consciously chosen activities aimed at improving the quality of the service is called the implementation strategy. The elements mentioned above are incorporated in it.

A major theme of this book is *how* quality policy is put into effect in the introduction and implementation of quality programmes. Active involvement of top management, ample mobilization of middle management, information meetings, training programmes, a facilitating management style, and especially the early involvement of the line organization: these are all indications of the desired implementation style. Our consulting experience in some 50 projects points in this direction.

Recently we have been approached by organizations that started on quality projects a few years ago which are stagnating now, partly due to the method of implementation. A new start is imperative – but the costs, including social and psychological costs, will be higher than those of the initial project. More successful projects show, however, that improving the quality of service is a stimulating experience.

In essence, quality improvement means creating a *learning organization*. The producer of services learns from the customers; the organizational units learn from one another; and management learns from the employees. This all results in everyone learning to do their own job better.

SUMMARY OF ARGUMENTS

We now sum up this book in a somewhat different manner. Within the group of consultants who are involved in quality improvement projects in our firm, we have examined which overhead slide sheets we use to clarify the ins and outs of quality improvement. The sheets most widely recommended are presented here with a brief explanation.

Figure 20.1 reflects the heart of quality improvement. It is important

Essence of quality improvement

Draw up an improvement plan:

- Who are our (internal) customers?

- How well do we perform in their eyes?

- What can we do better?

- What improvement actions can we take?

FIGURE 20.1

to state this once again in all its simplicity. This is what it is all about, this and nothing else. It also becomes clear that we are, in fact, talking about the continued existence and competitive power of the organization. Performing towards the customer, preferably better than the competitors! That is the whole story.

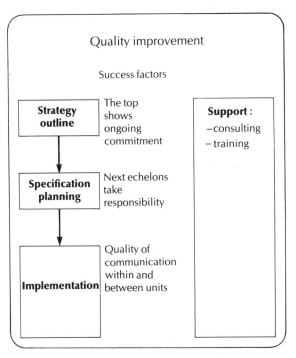

FIGURE 20.2

Figure 20.2 concerns the issue of change management, and it is in fact the most difficult question. The problem is not so much determining what we want to achieve, but getting a clear idea of *how*! That is another matter! This is a key question. Nearly all the chapters contain elements of this. Chapters 14, 18 and 19 provide an elaborate description and explanation of this model of change management. The box 'Support' is clarified specifically in part II, 'Supporting models and techniques', and in part IV, 'Motivation and improved cooperation'.

Figure 20.3 lists the areas which will need attention during implementation. In general these problems are solved in the course of the regular process of management and team meetings at the various levels. However, short work conferences are frequently needed to clear away the obstacles by means of specific input and training. The numbers in the

Quality improvement:
fields of attention during implementation

	Structure, strategy (goals)	Information (feedback)	Culture (correction)
Per unit (optimization)	Clarity of own products and tasks 10, 12	Results Costs 5, 8	Effective team communication 15, 17
Between units (process improvement)	Clarity of internal customers and customer success factors 9, 10	Customer success factors 5, 8, 9 ,10	(Internal) customer orientation Effective interface communication 6, 9, 17
The organization (organizational improvement)	Clarity of core business, goals and success factors 1, 7, 13	Results Competitive position 1, 7	The learning organization Exchange, learning from one another 2, 3, 16

FIGURE 20.3

figure indicate which chapters provide specific information. Regarding the interrelation between the key areas of strategy, structure, information and culture used in this figure, and their application both at the unit level and the organizational level, we refer you to chapters 2 and 3.

A fourth way to summarize the major aspects of our approach is expressed in figure 20.4. This sheet expresses that the main propelling force is a strategy of raising quality levels and customer satisfaction, driven by continuous feedback and performance measurement. The arrow 'Visibly improving results' expresses this force. Chapters 5, 7, 8 and 9 provide more information on this subject.

While you are working on improving results, two other areas will invariably start claiming attention. One is that existing obstacles and internal problems must be removed; you can find some helpful pointers on how to tackle this in chapters 4 and 10. The other is that communication must be improved; chapters 15 and 17 are devoted to this topic. In chapter 19 the tracks are integrated in the process of quality improvement.

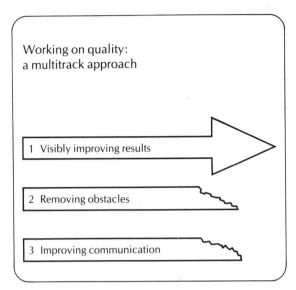

FIGURE 20.4

CONCLUSIONS

This book describes a diversity of practical means and aids in parts II and III. In addition, major developments are indicated concerning organizations in part I and the approach to quality improvement in part V. In part IV, separate attention is given to the important issues of quality of communication, motivation and action learning.

We wish to conclude by selecting a few of the recommendations, which together reflect an important development in the field of quality improvement as we have experienced it in our projects from 1983 to the present day:

1 Keep the approach simple: use a straightforward step-by-step plan, and avoid too much fuss.
2 Start with the customers! Some systematic attention to the customers' opinion on products and services is a good start.
3 Try to ingrain this more systematic feedback of (internal) customer signals into the organization's systems and procedures.
4 Involve the line organization from the start. The line is responsible for developing quality and customer orientation. Do not use a parallel organization of a steering committee, quality coordinators

and project groups to be in charge and responsible for quality improvement.

5 Pay separate attention to the quality of cooperation and communication.

6 Adjustments concerning strategy, structure, culture and information systems of the organization will gradually become apparent. Implement them when acceptance and support are sufficiently developed.

7 A process orientation raises motivation, while control and checking results make people defensive and promote resistance. Facilitating the process is something entirely different from calling people to account.

8 View working on quality and customer orientation more in terms of a gradual and continuing reorientation of management and performance, and less in terms of a project.

Index